An Illustrated History of
WORCESTER WOODS COUNTRY PARK

MARTI
Acres
1426 - 871

Newtown Grange

Nunnery Wood

Nunnery Farm

An Illustrated History of
WORCESTER WOODS COUNTRY PARK

by
Tanya Feasey

An Illustrated History of Worcester Woods Country Park
Tanya Feasey

Published by Aspect Design 2019
Malvern, Worcestershire, United Kingdom.

Designed, printed and bound by Aspect Design
89 Newtown Road, Malvern, Worcs. WR14 1PD
United Kingdom
Tel: 01684 561567
E-mail: allan@aspect-design.net
Website: www.aspect-design.net

All Rights Reserved.

Copyright © 2019 Tanya Feasey

Tanya Feasey has asserted her moral right
to be identified as the author of this work.

The right of Tanya Feasey to be identified as the author
of this work has been asserted in accordance with
Section 77 of the Copyright, Designs and Patents Act 1988.

This book is sold subject to the condition that it shall not, by way of trade or otherwise, be lent, resold, hired out or otherwise circulated without the publisher's prior consent in any form of binding or cover other than that in which it is published and without a similar condition including this condition being imposed on the subsequent purchaser.

A copy of this book has been deposited with the British Library Board

Cover Design Copyright © 2019 Aspect Design
Original photographs used with kind permission of Worcestershire Archive,
The Ordnance Survey, Robert & Beth Low, Jane Pond, and Tessa Kay Copyright © 2019

ISBN 978-1-912078-83-7

Contents

Introduction..7
    Overview..8
    Early History..8
    Ridge and Furrow...9
    Marl Pits..11
    Medieval Drainage System.....................................11
    Ditch and Bank Boundary.....................................11

The Four Farms...13
    Hornhill Farm..15
    Nunnery Farm, the Pitcher Family and the Little Comberton Connection......18
    Benjamin Fieldhouse..21

The Parker Brothers and the Little Comberton Connection......25
    William Parker..26
    John Parker...27
    The Pitcher family and many generations of George......29
    Worcestershire Corporation and Farming via Committee......34

Nunnery Wood..36

Newtown Grange...40
    John Herbert 'Bertie' Somer..................................44

Swinesherd Farm and the Watson Family...................47

Farming life in the Victorian and Edwardian era.........55
    Life on the farms...55
    Staff and families...57
    Crime..58
    Industrial Accidents..59

Modern Day...61

References..67
Illustrations..70

Introduction

This book started off as a project to produce a number of interpretation panels depicting the history of Worcester Woods Country Park. When this idea was floated I realised that despite working at Worcester Woods Country Park for well over a decade, I knew hardly anything about its history. I readily volunteered to help out with the project and after one session at the Worcestershire Archives, I was hooked!

I quickly ended up with far too much information to present on the interpretation boards. The boards went up with a potted history displayed upon them but I realised that I still had so much information that I couldn't present. With colleagues, volunteers and the general public presenting me with more and more information as interest in the project grew, I realised that the only way to present the information in its fullest form was in the guise of a book. So the idea for *The Illustrated History of Worcester Woods Country Park* was born.

Overview

Worcester Woods Country Park is based in the East of Worcester City. It is situated on Wildwood Drive of the A4440 and was established in 1979. The park consists of Nunnery Wood Local Nature Reserve, Hornhill Meadows Local Nature Reserve and other land. The visitor centre which is known as the Countryside Centre stands on the middle near the car park. Worcester Woods Country Park is about 38 hectares (100 acres) in size and is a popular visitor attraction in Worcester.

In the past, before Worcester Woods became a Country Park, it consisted of Nunnery Wood and agricultural land. It was believed that at some point before the medieval period Nunnery Wood was part of Feckenham Forest which could have covered the wider area before being cleared for agricultural land. By the late 1700s the agricultural land was formed by four farms, which spread out from beyond the Country Park boundary. They were; Nunnery Farm, Newtown Grange, Hornhill Farm and Swinesherd Mill Farm. Over time these four farms receded as land was sold off and developed and the remaining area was preserved as recreation land for the people of Worcester as Worcester Woods Country Park.

The Country Park first came into being in October 1979[3] with Hereford and Worcestershire County Council (Now Worcestershire County Council) acquiring Nunnery Wood and the fields that currently contain the Countryside Centre. By 1984[3] Worcester Woods had officially been designated a Country Park. The Countryside Centre opened in July 1987[3]. In 1990[3] Hornhill Meadows and some of the adjoining fields were purchased making up the the Country Park that we have today.

Early History.

An Archaeological Landscape Survey of Worcester Woods Country Park was undertaken in 2004[5] and this is the basis for what we know about the pre medieval history of the area, as there are no written accounts from this time.

The oldest known sign of human habitation in Worcester Woods Country Park is a sub rectangular enclosure, which is only visible from the air as a crop mark in the furthermost easterly field. This crop mark is clearly visible in pre 1980s aerial photographs[5], before scrub was allowed to encroach upon the area.

The crop mark is thought to date from the late prehistoric to the Roman period and could have been a settlement or a farmstead. No excavation has been undertaken of the crop mark to date, so no more accurate information is available about its origins.

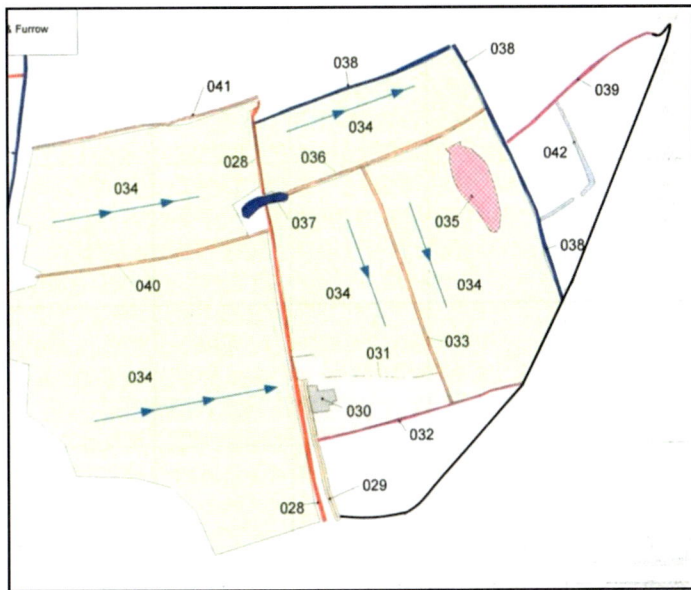

Fig. 1: Hornhill Meadows Archaeology map[5]. The crop mark can be seen on the top right as an L shaped grey mark. Also marked is the large marl pit in pink and the direction of the ridge and furrow shown by the arrowed lines.

Ridge and Furrow.

There is then a large time gap in the archaeological timeline until the medieval period where several surviving features can be seen around Worcester Woods Country Park.

The most common of these features are the Ridge and Furrow Earthworks. These features can be seen today as undulations that run across the fields, like corrugations in cardboard. These distinctive undulations are formed by a type of non-reversible plough that was used on the same piece of land. Over the years more ploughing formed a more pronounced ridge and furrow. The ridges were where the soil was deposited and the furrows were where the plough removed soil. Most Ridge and Furrow earthworks date from the middle ages with the method being phased out in the 1600s.

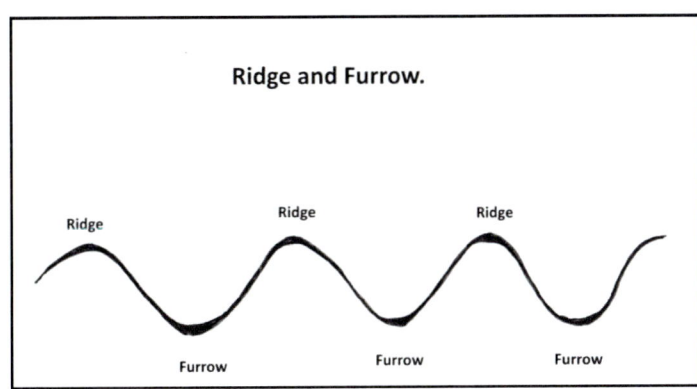

Fig. 2: An illustration showing the undulations caused by ridge and furrow ploughing patterns.

Ridge and Furrow can be seen clearly in Hornhill Meadows, but is also visible in the middle of Nunnery Wood. This shows us that in the medieval period both the woodland and farmland areas were farmed. At some point farming was abandoned in the area where Nunnery Wood now stands and this was allowed to revert back to woodland. It is thought this happened around the 1300s[5] although no written accounts exist.

Fig. 3: Photo showing the ridge and furrow in Hornhill Meadows during the winter. The snow has melted on top of the ridges, only settling in the furrows.

Fig. 4: Photo of the pond in Nunnery Wood which was previously a marl pit, but now holds water. The ditch in the foreground is part of a later medieval drainage ditch system that runs through the wood.

Marl Pits.

Another feature which you can see throughout Worcester Woods Country Park are a number of medieval marl pits. Marl is the name given to a nutrient-rich clay which was dug out of the ground and used to fertilise crops. The removal of the marl formed deep hollows in the ground and these remain visible up to the present day. The woodland pond in the middle of Nunnery Wood is an old marl pit which now holds water. There are also several dry marl pits on the North-Eastern edge of Nunnery Wood and one in Hornhill Meadows. Having several Marl pits in Nunnery Wood gives weight to the theory that the woodland was once agricultural land.

Medieval Drainage System.

A prominent archaeological feature, which can be seen throughout Nunnery Wood, is the Medieval ditch and bank system used to mark the woodland boundary. A series of drainage ditches run from the higher end of Nunnery Wood in the north through to the lowest corner in the south west near County Hall Lakes. This provides drainage through the woodlands and also feeds the woodland pond. The drainage ditches in the middle of the woods are still in use for this purpose today and can be seen performing their function well after heavy rain.

Ditch and Bank Boundary.

The ditch and bank boundary is still visible today running around the edge of Nunnery Wood. This probably dates to the same time period as the medieval drainage ditch system, as one runs into the other at various locations. The ditch and bank boundary is where mud was removed, forming a ditch. The mud was piled up to form a bank adjacent to a ditch. This was a regularly used method of marking the boundary of land, as erecting and maintaining fences was a time consuming and costly activity.

The boundaries were also marked with old pollarded oak trees. Pollarding was a form of high cutting of trees to harvest wood (Fig. 7). The trees were pruned at height to stop farm animals and deer browsing the regrowth. A prominent example of an old boundary pollard is the old oak tree (Fig. 6), fenced off near the firewood pile on the north eastern boundary of Nunnery Wood but if you walk around the perimeter of Nunnery Wood you will regularly come across these veteran trees.

Fig. 5: A photo of the medieval ditch and bank which marks out the boundary of Nunnery Wood.

Fig. 6: The old boundary pollarded oak tree. This tree is approximately 400–500 years old.

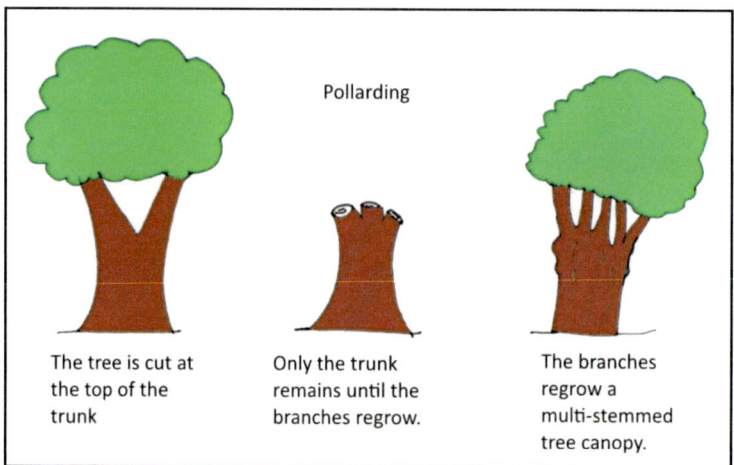

Fig. 7: An illustration showing pollarding techniques where trees are cut at the top of the trunk and then grow back in multi- stemmed form. These were often used as boundary markers.

The Four Farms

By the mid-1700s the land that is now Worcester Woods Country Park was covered by four farms: Hornhill Farm, Newtown Grange, Nunnery Farm and Swinesherd Mill (see Fig. 8). The farms probably dated back further but there are scarce written accounts before the 1700s so it is hard to accurately date them.

Hornhill Farm was the smallest at 11 acres and Swinesherd Mill the largest at 250 acres. Nunnery Farm and Newtown Grange were about 180 acres in size. The farms did change slightly in size with fields being added or sold off at various times until the 1930s when a depression in the farming sector led to hard times and caused an acceleration of land being sold off. These farms then slowly reduced in size until finally Nunnery Farm was the first farm to be sold in its entirety for building, followed by Newtown Grange, then Swinesherd and finally Hornhill Farm.

Most of these farms are now built upon with the surviving fields preserved to make up what is now Worcester Woods Country Park.

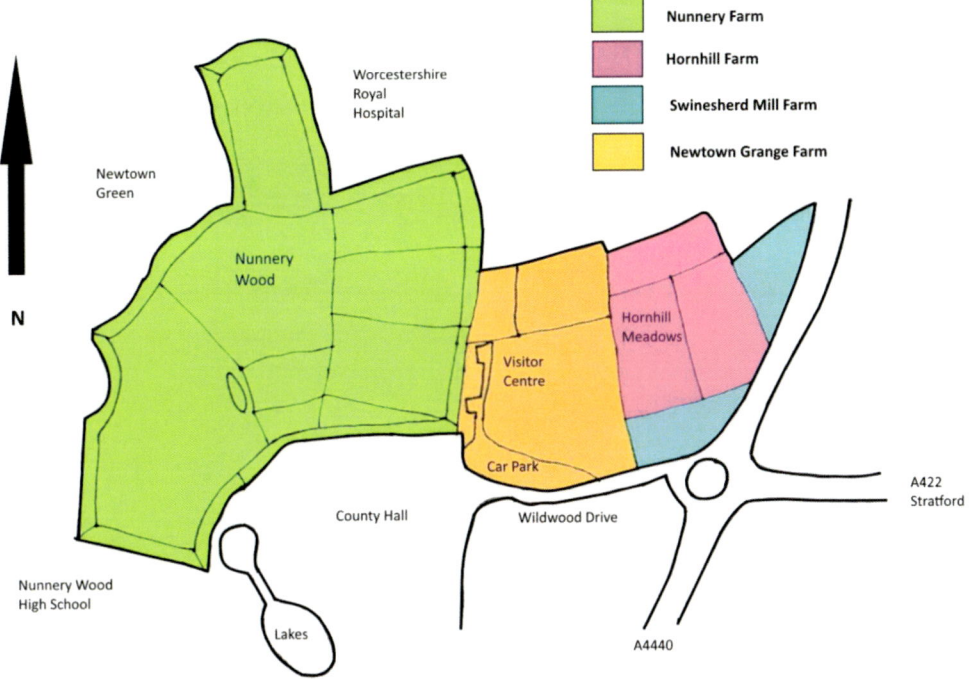

Fig. 8: Map of Worcester Woods Country Park showing the areas that were previously covered by the four different farms.

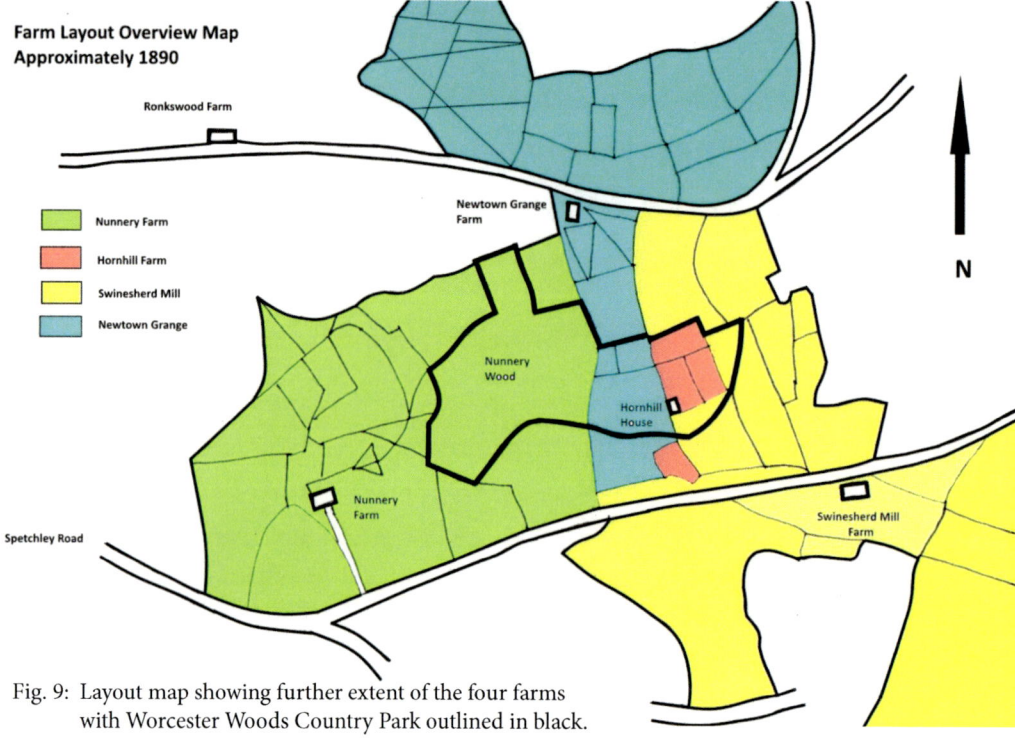

Fig. 9: Layout map showing further extent of the four farms with Worcester Woods Country Park outlined in black.

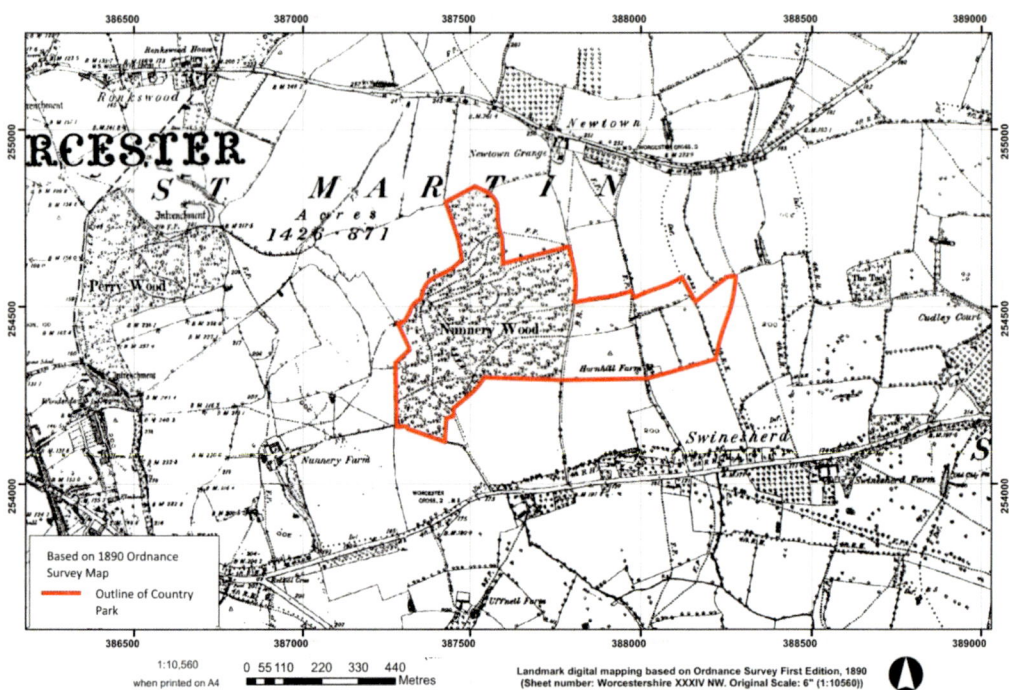

Fig. 10: 1890 O.S Map of the area with Worcester Woods Country Park outlined in red. The four farmhouses of Swinesherd, Nunnery, Hornhill and Newtown can also be seen on the map.

Hornhill Farm

The remains of Hornhill Farm can still be seen in Worcester Woods Country Park in the present day. It was a small farm of 11 acres which covered what is now known as Hornhill Meadows Local Nature Reserve. The farmhouse was situated in the corner of an old orchard and bricks and rubble remains can still be seen amongst the old fruit trees to this day. Evidence in the census and newspaper adverts show Hornhill farm would have been managed at times as a smallholding on its own and as part of the bigger surrounding farms. Looking at census returns shows many different tenants living in Hornhill House at different times and also many different land owners.

Fig. 11: Hornhill Farm detail (highlighted in red) of land owned in the 19th Century. Based on the 1890 OS Map.

The farmhouse dates back to 1764[2] although judging by the ridge and furrow patterns in Hornhill Meadows it was likely these meadows had been farmed long before Hornhill House was built.

One of the earliest references we can find giving any detail about Hornhill House is the sale of Hornhill Villa (as it was then called) in the Worcester Journal 1826[18]. At the time it was owned by Thomas Hill who was probably part of the Hill family, who owned a lot of land in the area. Hornhill Farm was being auctioned along with its entire contents including linen, bedding, a seven tine scuffler, a narrow wheeled waggon with thripples, several pikes, fourteen iron hairs, a cheese press, two pigs and poultry. There was no mention of the adjacent fields which now comprise Hornhill Meadows, so at the time these were probably owned separately and perhaps rented out to one of the surrounding farms.

By 1838 Hornhill Meadows was listed as part of Swinesherd Farm[9]. This was being farmed by John Watson who had been tenant of Nunnery Farm in 1836[11]. The 1839[104] tithe map gives Hornhill Farm as being owned by Thomas Ward with the tenant in the house being George Day. The surrounding meadows were still farmed by John Watson although George Day could have been in his employ.

By 1851 the census was giving Hornhill House as being uninhabited. In 1855 we find the first mention of John Tustin being at Hornhill House, with him being listed in a Worcester trade directory[19] as being a farmer in residence at Hornhill Villa.

In 1857 Hornhill Farm was sold[20]. The Worcestershire Chronicle had an advert for Hornhill house and meadow *'A capital meadow house, two stall stable, piggeries, detached cow house, shed, fold yard, also neat flower and kitchen garden.'* The advert also stated the land and 11 acres of fields were being rented out to John Tustin. John Tustin then gets mentioned again in 1861 on the census. He is living at Hornhill Villa (house) with his wife Mary Ann, four children and three servants. By the 1871 census John Tustin had vacated Hornhill Farm and was now Farming at Ronkswood Farm and living next to Ronkswood House. Ronkswood House can still be seen standing on Newtown Road as a large white building half way up the hill. John Tustin was mentioned[2] as being a coal merchant known as 'Gentleman Tustin'. He was described as handsome and well groomed. He captured the affections of a baronet's daughter but the family put a stop to it because of his unacceptable occupation!!

In 1867 Johnathan Jackson is listed as owning Hornhill Farm[10], with his name occurring on the Newtown Farm map as an adjacent landowner. (A lot of old maps give names of all the neighbouring landowners and sometimes tenants which can be a very valuable source of information.)

In 1871 it was being farmed by cattle dealer Harvey Smith who lived there with his wife Elizabeth and two servants. Johnathan Jackson, who had previously brought the farm, was father to Elizabeth, wife of Harvey Smith and therefore Harvey Smith's father in law. By 1879 Harvey Smith was listed in a local trade directory[21] as farming both Newtown Grange and Ronkswood Farms, living next door to John Tustin at Ronkswood Farm.

In 1884 Hornhill Farm was sold again[22], this time to a Thomas Wheeler of Kemerton for £1450. An article appeared in 1885 in the Worcester Journal[23] showing that Thomas Wheeler was letting out Hornhill House and 11 acres. At the time it was being rented to Edwin Watson who had retired there from Swinesherd Farm. By 1891 Edwin Watson had died, and according to the census, John Cooper, who worked as a signalman on the railway, was living at Hornhill House with his wife Eliza and three children, two of whom worked as general labourers, and also his niece and a lodger. During this time a lot of work was taking place installing railway lines in the area, and this was reflected in local census returns, showing many people had changed occupation from farm labourers to railway workers. The railways obviously provided a lot of work for the local population and certainly at that time more dwellings seemed to be popping up in the area to reflect this. In 1892 Hornhill House was for sale again[24]. By then Thomas Wheeler

Fig. 12: Still visible. Old wall by the ditch in front of Hornhill House.

Fig. 13: Rubble remains of Hornhill House by the old orchard.

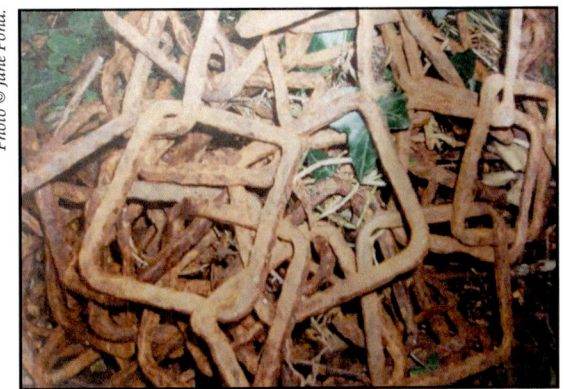

Fig. 14: Old chain harrow remains found whilst renovating Hornhill Orchard in 2005.

had died and his estate was being sold off. An article which was a report of the auction of Hornhill house stated *'There was good attendance at the auction. Bidding started at £500 and went to Mr Benjamin Perkins at £1150.'* It is likely that Benjamin Perkins then rented it out again to various tenants.

In 1901, according to the census, another tenant was given as living at Hornhill Farm. Alexander Hadley a farmer, lived at the house with his wife Esther and three daughters. It is not known if Alexander Hadley was farming Hornhill Meadows at the time although with his occupation being given as farmer, it may have been likely.

By the 1911 census Hornhill House had another occupant in Jessie Turner who was a butcher and farmer by occupation. This was quite common in this era, as smallholders tended to farm a small area, raising a few farm animals, and then engaging in part time butchery to sell-on some of the livestock for a small profit. Jesse Turner lived at Hornhill House with his wife Eliza and two sons Alfred and Robert who both worked on the farm. They also had a daughter and one servant living with them.

Hornhill house was demolished in the 1950s after lying vacant for a time. According to legend in the 1980s rangers at Worcester Woods Country Park found an intact well under the Hornhill House rubble. This was seen as a hazard and the rest of the house rubble was used to infill the well to stop people falling into it. The rubble is still visible and can be seen clearly in winter, when the vegetation has died back, in the corner of the old orchard.

Nunnery Farm, the Pitcher Family and the Little Comberton Connection.

Nunnery Farm was originally part of the Nunnery owned by the White Ladies Nuns, a Cistercian order of nuns who were based at Whitstones Priory north of Worcester[4]. The White Ladies Nuns were also granted land at Aston which then became known as White Ladies Aston. It was also very likely they owned Nunnery Wood. As the White Ladies date back to 1255, it is possible that Nunnery Farm dated back towards this time although we have no documentary evidence to say when it was established. Nunnery Farm would have been managed to produce food and timber for the running of the priory. In 1536 following the dissolution of the monasteries by Henry VIII, the Nunnery was taken off the nuns along with its land holdings. We know that in 1544 the previous land holdings of the nunnery at White Ladies Aston, were given to Thomas Hill, who kept it in the Hill family, with the land being passed down to various members. I have found reference to the Hill family with regard to Nunnery Farm in the 1700s so it is possible that this was given to the Hill family at the same time as White Ladies Aston in 1544.

Nunnery Farm was rented to tenants, sometimes with the farmhouse and farmland being let separately. Nunnery farmhouse was built in the 1700s. The Victoria County History of Worcester[4] states that the farm was a *'two storey early 18th Century brick house with a 19th Century three storey edition.'* A 1772 map of Worcestershire by Isaac Taylor[97] clearly shows Nunnery Wood and a building known as 'The Nunnery' approximately where Nunnery Farm once stood. (Nunnery Farm was often referred to as just 'The Nunnery') An exact build date is not known but there are certainly frequent references to the farm by the late 1700s.

It would not have been the first version of Nunnery Farm to exist, likely replacing an older farmhouse. It is not known whether the old farmhouse was based on the site of the latest farmhouse.

Fig. 15: An artist's impression of what Nunnery Farmhouse would have looked like in the early 20th Century. The painting was recreated from old black and white photos showing the demolition of Nunnery Farm and descriptions of the farm. You can see clearly that the farm was made up of two distinct halves, with the earlier red-brick 18th century part at the back and the later 19th century white three story addition at the front.

There is a field named 'Old Nunnery' on the North Western edge of Nunnery Wood (see map). Whether this field name refers to a previous house location or perhaps a previous extension of Nunnery Wood is unknown and we can only speculate upon the location of an older farmhouse.

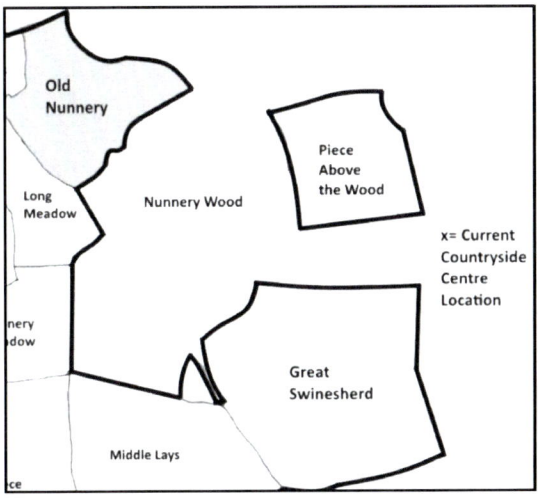

Fig. 16: Detail of Nunnery Farm Map (1850s) with the field named Old Nunnery on the top left hand side of Nunnery Wood (shaded) - where Newtown Green is now situated.

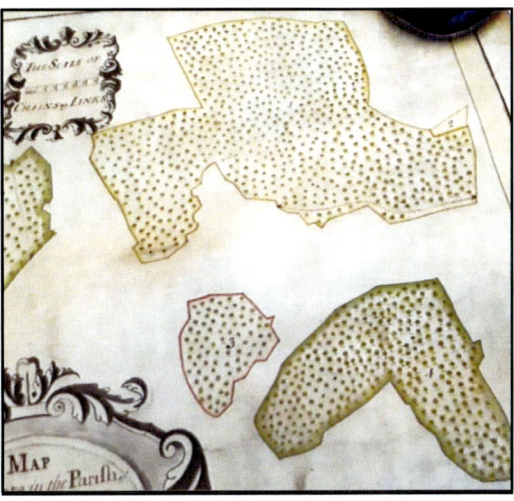

Fig. 17: 1751 Map: Detail showing Nunnery Wood, top right hand corner[94] The northern tip of the wood is facing towards the left on this map.

During the 1700s several names crop up in relation to Nunnery Farm. The Hill Family are mentioned in 'Historic Worcester Streets'[1]. They were a family of wealthy farmers and lawyers who lived at Ronkswood House and farmed 1000 acres of land in the area. Certainly on old maps Nunnery Farm and Ronkswood Farm were farmed together it seems under the same ownership[6,7] with the farmhouse being rented separately, and we know that Hornhill Farm was owned by Thomas Hill when it was sold in 1826. A 1751[94] road map of Nunnery Wood and Ronkswood Farm has the land down as belonging to Richard Hawkins and William Russell but they could have been tenants at the time.

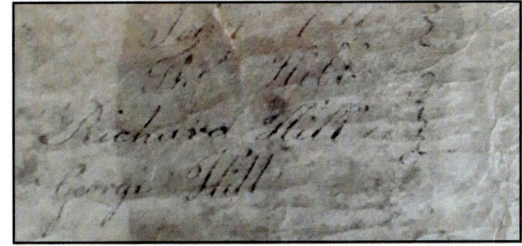

Fig. 18: Detail from the back of the 1790 map. Very faded handwriting but you can just make out the Hill family.

A 1790 map of the area[7] includes Nunnery Farm and Woods and again mentions Mr Russell as the owner of the roads surrounding the farm. It does not mention directly who owns Nunnery Farm at the time, as the map was drawn up to show road ownership. Curiously, on the back of the map is some very faded writing which lists various members of the Hill Family (Richard, George, John and Thomas Hill.) plus some other people Maybe they were the landowners and

Mr Russell was the tenant. Often the farms were run by one tenant, whilst the farmhouses were lived in by another tenant and fields and houses were often sub-let, confusing matters even more.

An article in Berrow's Journal in 1794 announces the death of Miss Dorothy Best aged eighteen, the daughter of Mr Best of Nunnery Farm[83]. The following year, again in Berrows Journal[84] an announcement was made of the death of Dorothy's father, Mr Francis Best. They were probably renting the farmhouse, separate to the farm at the time, which still appeared to be farmed as part of Ronkswood Farm. The Bests are mentioned on the 1790[7] map as tenants who rented a field just south of Nunnery Farm on the other side of Spetchley Road. This would have likely been used as a smallholding providing food for the family at the farmhouse.

Although no further mention of the Hill family or the Best family can be found in relation

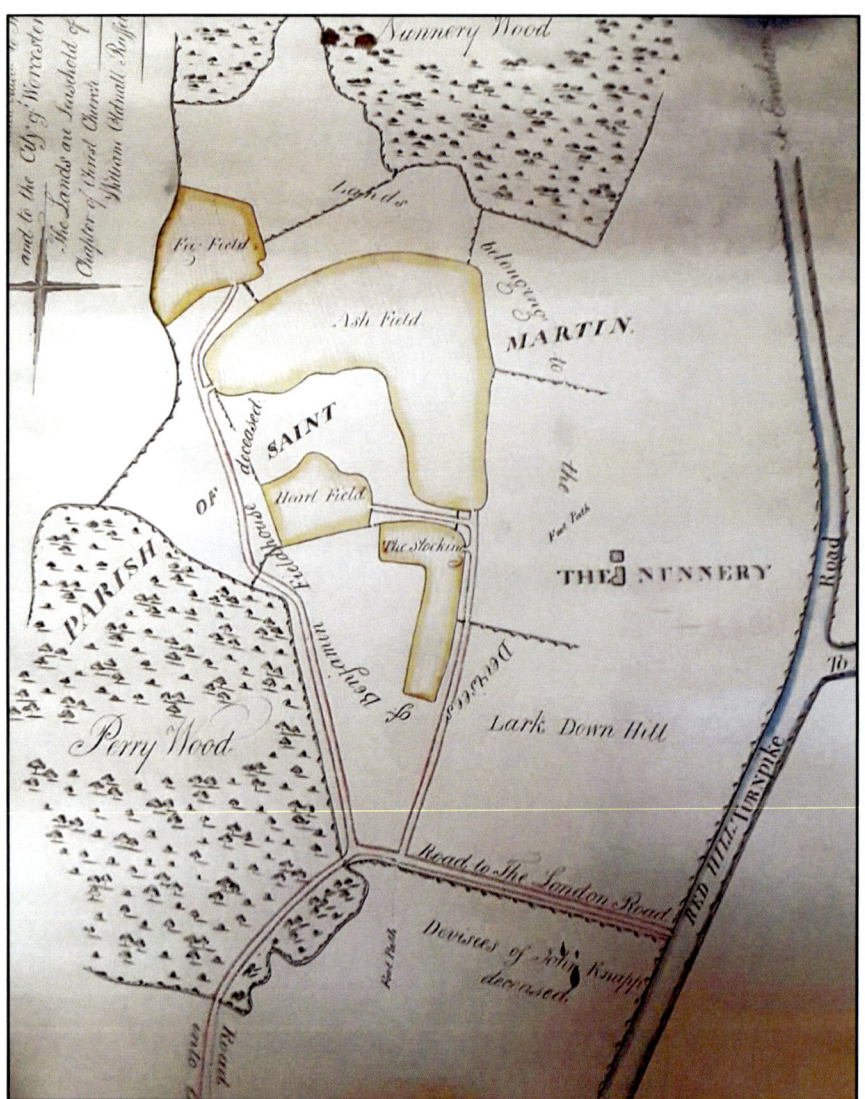

Fig. 19: Detail from the 1824 map of the Nunnery Farm area[8]. Nunnery Farm is stated as being 'The Nunnery' on the map.

to Nunnery Farm, the Russell family still had involvement with the farm. Another road map this time drawn up in 1824[8] shows William Oldnall Russell as the lessee, leasing land from Christchurch College (possibly Nunnery Wood). The middle portion of land on this map, which contains several Nunnery Fields; Feg field, Ash field, Heart field and The Stocking. These all belonged to the estate of Mr Benjamin Fieldhouse who had passed away in about 1820. The map doesn't show precisely which bits William Oldnall Russell owned, but from the map it looks likely he was also renting Nunnery and Perry Wood at this time.

Benjamin Fieldhouse

After Francis Best's passing we are unsure of who took on rental of the farm next but by 1813 it was in the ownership of a Mr Benjamin Fieldhouse. Benjamin Fieldhouse was a notable Worcester publican and wealthy landowner. According to information given by former city Journalist and historian Bob Blandford[98], he owned the Star and Garter Inn (later the Star Inn) and was also licensee of the Hop Pole Inn (this stood next door to the Star and Garter) and owned a large chunk of The Crown Inn. Certainly by 1813 he was trying to sell the farm. At this time we also find an interesting article in the Worcester Journal[25] about a red cow. *'Stolen or strayed from lands near Nunnery Farm last night or early this morning. A large red cow of Hereford breed with wide horns, very fresh'*. A reward of ten guineas was offered by Mr B Fieldhouse of the Hop Pole Inn.

In 1813 Nunnery Farm was advertised in the Worcester Journal[26] as *'To be sold by private contract'*. At the time it was referred to as *'The Nunnery'* which seems more common in earlier references to the farm. The sale notice states *'This estate is in the holding of Mr Benjamin Fieldhouse who will appoint a person to show it. N.B If The Nunnery is not sold by private contract before 1st September next, it will be offered for sale by auction in various lots.'*

The sale was unsuccessful and in 1814 part of the farm appears for sale again[27]. This time in lots along with other parcels of land and houses also owned by Mr Fieldhouse but not relating to Nunnery Farm.

The farm remained unsold but for some reason, Mr Fieldhouse did not follow up on his offer to break the farm up and sell it in lots. By 1821 Benjamin Fieldhouse had died. But the farm was still part of his estate and was now being offered for sale once again. It appears in the Hereford Journal[28] where it is described as being *'late in the occupation of Mr Benjamin Fieldhouse, deceased.'*

By 1824 the farm was still unsold and appeared for sale again in the Worcester Journal[29]. It was described as *'Consisting of a good dwelling house fit for residence of a respectable family. Barn, sheds, stable, granary, wainhouse. Spacious folds and rickyards, large and productive gardens, well planted with choice sorts of fruit trees.'*

Another notice in August 1824 also advertised growing crops of Nunnery Farm for sale in the Worcester Journal[30] selling 55 acres of wheat and 23 acres of beans. This shows that despite the fact the farm was for sale, a tenant must have still been working the farm.

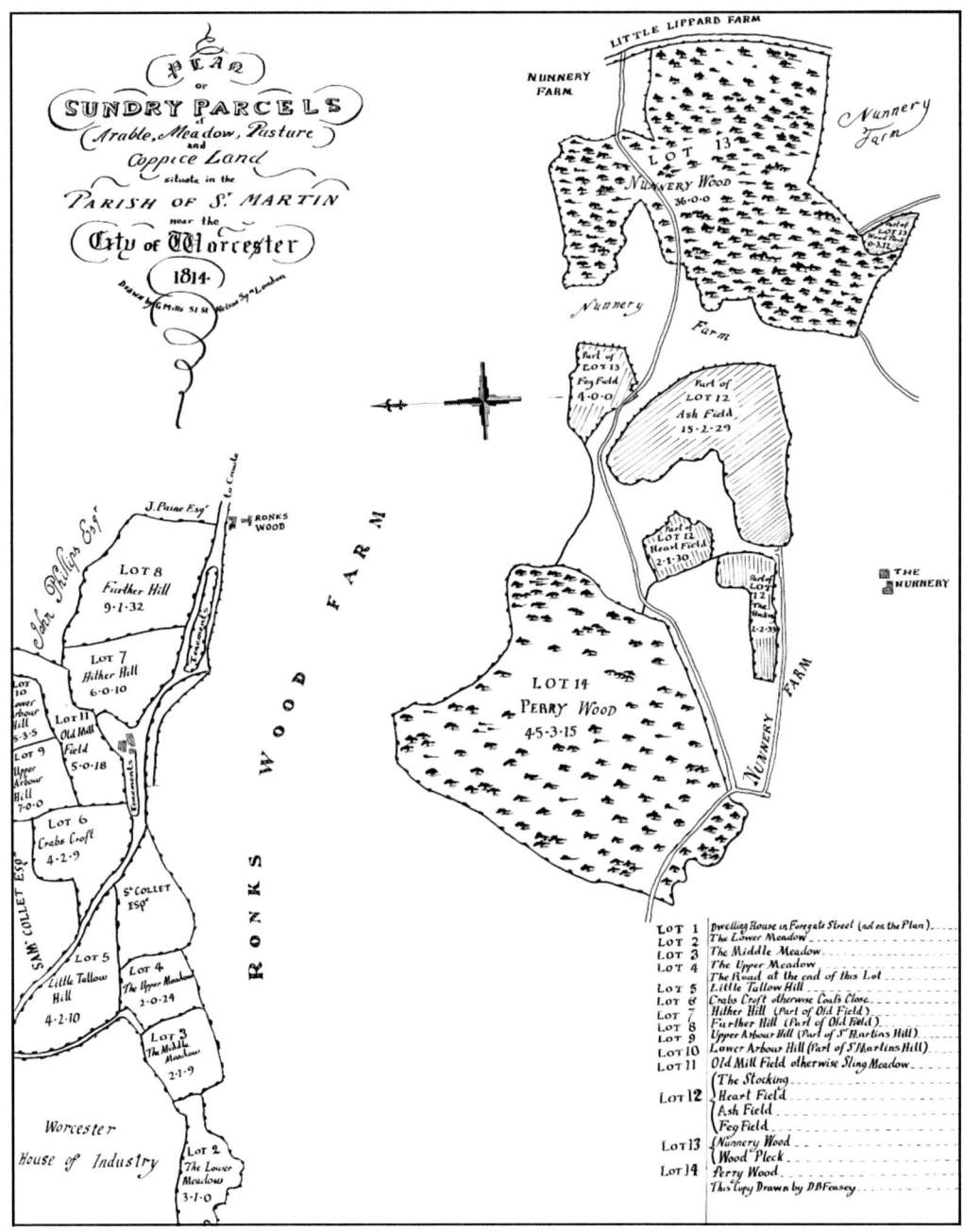

Fig. 20: A copy made from a badly damaged 1814 map of the Nunnery Farm and Ronkswood Estate land being sold by Benjamin Fieldhouse. North is shown facing to the left. Credit David Feasey.

The farm remained unsold after this point and then went into the occupation of the Oliver family who were mentioned in documents relating to Mr Fieldhouse, so were probably his heirs. An article in the Worcester Journal in 1826[31] stated that W A Oliver Esq died aged 66 at Nunnery Farm. His widow remained at the farmhouse, and in 1829 another article appeared in the Worcester Journal[32] mentioning a Mr John Taylor being caught for stealing five pigs, property of Mrs Oliver of Nunnery Farm. He was sentenced to twelve months hard labour. This shows that the Oliver family were farming in the area to some extent, even if it was just a few fields and a smallholding, with the rest of Nunnery Farm being rented out.

By 1832 the effects of Mrs Oliver were being sold from Nunnery Farm. The sale mentioned in the Worcester Journal[33] included *'Livestock, hay, implements and c, consisting of three capital waggons, geldings, and three in-calving cows, excellent milkers...'* Additionally, also mentioned were: *'Two large ricks of well ended hay to go off, two broad waggons, three broad wheeled carts, wood roll, ploughs, harrows, an excellent winnowing machine, sieves and riddles.'*

The list of furniture included *'a handsome four poster mahogany bed, hair mattresses, well-seasoned bedding, blankets, Marseilles quilts, cotton counter panes, an excellent mahogany wardrobe and chest of drawers.'*

When Mrs Oliver was selling her effects it is unknown if she had died or was moving away. We do know that after this date John Watson took on the farm for a short period. He was tenant there in 1836 when the farm went up for sale[11]. John Watson also farmed at Swinesherd Farm and his family went on to become established there for the next 100 years after leaving Nunnery Farm.

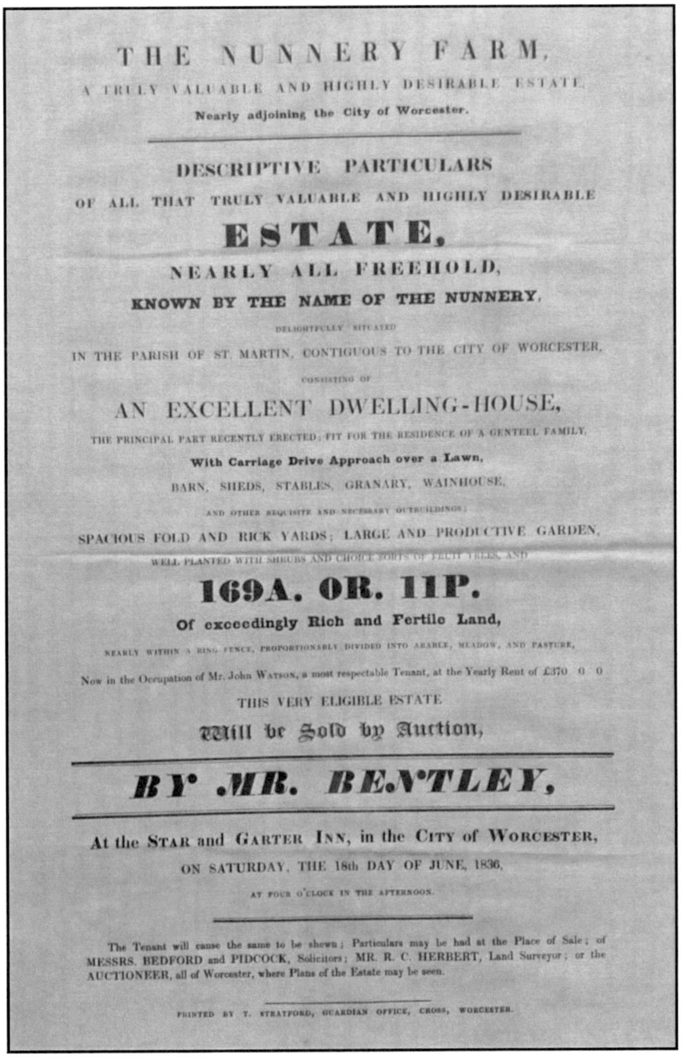
THE NUNNERY FARM,
A TRULY VALUABLE AND HIGHLY DESIRABLE ESTATE,
Nearly adjoining the City of Worcester.

DESCRIPTIVE PARTICULARS
OF ALL THAT TRULY VALUABLE AND HIGHLY DESIRABLE
ESTATE,
NEARLY ALL FREEHOLD,
KNOWN BY THE NAME OF THE NUNNERY,
DELIGHTFULLY SITUATED
IN THE PARISH OF ST. MARTIN, CONTIGUOUS TO THE CITY OF WORCESTER,
CONSISTING OF
AN EXCELLENT DWELLING-HOUSE,
THE PRINCIPAL PART RECENTLY ERECTED; FIT FOR THE RESIDENCE OF A GENTEEL FAMILY,
With Carriage Drive Approach over a Lawn,
BARN, SHEDS, STABLES, GRANARY, WAINHOUSE,
AND OTHER REQUISITE AND NECESSARY OUTBUILDINGS;
SPACIOUS FOLD AND RICK YARDS; LARGE AND PRODUCTIVE GARDEN,
WELL PLANTED WITH SHRUBS AND CHOICE SORTS OF FRUIT TREES, AND
169A. 0R. 11P.
Of exceedingly Rich and Fertile Land,
NEARLY WITHIN A RING FENCE, PROPORTIONABLY DIVIDED INTO ARABLE, MEADOW, AND PASTURE,
Now in the Occupation of Mr. John Watson, a most respectable Tenant, at the Yearly Rent of £370 0 0
THIS VERY ELIGIBLE ESTATE
Will be Sold by Auction,
BY MR. BENTLEY,
At the Star and Garter Inn, in the City of Worcester,
ON SATURDAY, THE 18th DAY OF JUNE, 1836,
AT FOUR O'CLOCK IN THE AFTERNOON.

The Tenant will cause the same to be shewn; Particulars may be had at the Place of Sale; of MESSRS. BEDFORD and PIDCOCK, Solicitors; MR. R. C. HERBERT, Land Surveyor; or the AUCTIONEER, all of Worcester, where Plans of the Estate may be seen.

PRINTED BY T. STRATFORD, GUARDIAN OFFICE, CROSS, WORCESTER.

Fig. 21 Sale notice for Nunnery Farm in 1836.[11]

In June 1836 the estate was sold. It is thought that at this point the farm was bought by the Reverend William Parker and his brother John Parker. William Parker was Reverend at Little Comberton Church and John Parker was a solicitor in Worcester. Shortly after the sale, the farm was tenanted by Mr Thomas Porter, who was mentioned in 1838 when his daughter Charlotte aged eleven sadly died[99]. It was common for rich gentry to buy up land and farms, and then have a tenant installed to undertake the actual management of the land.

The tithe map of 1839[104] shows John Parker as being the owner of Nunnery Farm, and Thomas Porter as still being the tenant. A search in the Worcestershire Archives uncovered several bills and ledgers relating to Nunnery Farm[12]. It would appear, from the information given on these, that John Parker owned a third share in the farm, whilst William Parker owned two thirds. John Parker, who lived near Perry Wood, being the more local of the two brothers, dealt most with the day to day management of the farm and was often named on documents as the land owner with his brother's name being omitted.

In 1844 an advert appeared in the Worcestershire Chronicle about the effects of Mr Thomas Porter[100] *'who is quitting Nunnery Farm'* being sold at auction. The effects included farm animals and farm equipment and it seems likely that this is the year that the Pitcher family came to join the farm. From this point onwards Nunnery Farm stayed in the hands of various generations of the Pitcher family until it was sold in 1940.

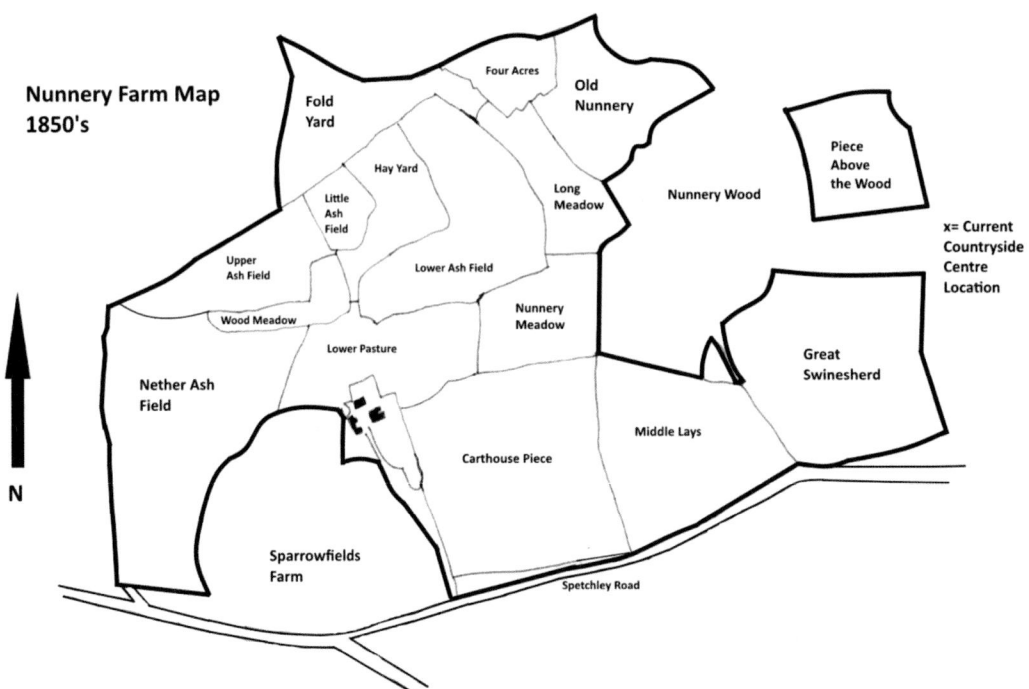

Fig. 22: Nunnery Farm with field names in the 1850s. Various Nunnery Farm maps show differing names for some of the fields so the field names did change over time[12].

The Parker Brothers and the Little Comberton Connection

As we know, in 1836 Nunnery Farm was brought by William and John Parker and it was likely they also took on the lease for Nunnery Wood at this time. The Parker brothers were very wealthy gentlemen who owned a lot of land throughout Worcestershire.

William Parker was the Reverend of Little Comberton Church near Pershore. John Parker Esq lived closer to Nunnery Farm at Woodside House in Red Hill, and was working as a solicitor at the time. The Pitcher Family were originally from the Little Comberton area and would have been previous tenant farmers of William Parker. They were an active part of Little Comberton church and many of them are buried in Little Comberton Churchyard.

There was a third Parker brother, the Reverend Charles Hubert Parker and he was Reverend at Great Comberton Church in the adjacent village to his brother William, but as far as I am aware he was not involved in the running of the Nunnery Farm Estate.

As the Pitchers were a large and well established farming family already known to William Parker when Thomas Porter gave up his tenancy of Nunnery Farm, it made perfect sense for them to take on the running of the farm for the Parker family and the decision seemed to work out well for the Parkers and the Pitchers. When George Pitcher moved to Worcester to manage Nunnery Farm most of his children, who were young adults at this, stage stayed in Little Comberton and continued farming. His son William Godwin Yeend Pitcher farmed a lot of land around Little Comberton and became one of the greatest agriculturalists of the era in Worcestershire[103].

Accounts can be seen in the Worcestershire Archives[12] of the rental set up between the Parkers and the Pitchers. Rental accounts from 1863 show rates being paid on Nunnery Wood, road rates, land taxes and income taxes. They were all split with two thirds being attributable to William Parker and a third to John Parker.

A letter dated March 1857 from Reverend William Parker to George Pitcher[12] states *'Taking in consideration the present high to late high and present food price of corn, we think in justice to ourselves that we are called upon to ask for a higher rent for Nunnery Farm.'*

The rent was increased to £320 per year paid in two instalments six months apart. William Parker ends his letter to George Pitcher telling him he deserves *'every credit for the management of the farm.'*

At the time farms were doing very well with high prices being paid for corn, and a new type of affluent gentleman farmer class was emerging as a result. This boom period lasted well into the 1870s and farms profited and expanded during this period.

William Parker

William Parker was born in 1793 in Tamworth. He was the son of William Parker Esq and Mary Parker. He went to Trinity College Oxford[34] where he graduated with an MA in 1818.

In 1822 he married Jane Paget at Loughborough who was the only child of John Paget the younger of Loughborough. She came from a wealthy family and the marriage settlement revealed that that she was endowed with one share of the River Soar Navigation Trust plus £4000 in one annuity fund and a further £3600 in another annuity fund to be split between her and her children[86]. William and Jane went on to have at least five daughters Mary, Jane, Anne, Katherine and Marianne. Sadly William Parker survived three of his daughters with Katherine only living until 16, Mary only living to 20 and Anne who died aged fifty-two. His wife Anne died in 1870 aged sixty-nine. It is not thought that William Parker remarried thereafter[35].

In 1826 he became rector of Little Comberton, and he stayed rector there until his death in 1884, serving the church for a total of fifty eight years[34]. His brother, Charles Hubert Parker, also became rector of Great Comberton church at the same time until his death in 1883[36].

Fig. 23: Little Comberton Church, with the Pitcher family graves in the foreground leading up to the front door. Credit Jane Pond.

William Parker was also noted in Crockfords as being the curator at Elmley Castle and assistant curator at Wick[36].

In 1836, or thereabouts, William Parker, along with his brother John, bought Nunnery Farm. William Parker owned a two-thirds share with John owning a one third share.

According to his obituary[34] William Parker was a keen fossil collector, and by his death had amassed an amazing collection of fossils, which he found on his frequent walks up Bredon Hill. He was also a very keen naturalist and pomologist (fruit cultivation: particularly apples). He was very well thought of in the local community, being generous to charities and his parishioners. It was said he had managed over 100 bank books for his parishioners (often people were illiterate and found it hard to have bank accounts as a result). He was a wealthy man and he endowed some of the church bells and the tower clock to Little Comberton Church. By the time he grew old, his daughter Anne had moved back into the rectory with him. Anne was widowed and lived there with her daughter Caroline, probably caring for William Parker after his wife's death. Anne Barker (Barker being her married name) lived with William Parker until her death two years before his passing.

Fig. 24: Dave Saunders at Little Comberton Church in 2018, demonstrating the winding mechanisms of the church clock, which was endowed to the church by Rev William Parker.

Fig. 25: Photo of one of the bells in Little Comberton Church tower. The bells were given to the church by an endowment made by Rev William Parker.

William Parker died in 1884 and left everything to two of his nephews Francis Parker and William Parker Howell[35]. His estate was valued at £63,881 11s 11d and would have included Nunnery Farm. It is not known for how long the nephews held onto these estates, but sometime later Nunnery Farm was sold to George Pitcher.

John Parker

John Parker was born in 1799. By the 1851 census he was a resident at Woodside House in Larkhill, where he remained until his death. By this time he was working as a solicitor and was married to his wife Charlotte Paget Parker. He had four children, Mary, Francis, John Paget and William Henry[35]. He had entered the legal profession in 1819 and served as a solicitor in Worcester until his retirement in 1870. In 1872, two years into his retirement, he was appointed magistrate for Worcester and became Deputy

Lieutenant of the County. In his obituary[37] it was stated that the Parker family were descended from the Cromwells, although I have found no evidence to directly support the claim.

Fig. 26: View from Perry Wood over Woodside towards Worcester –dated 1819. [85]

John Parker's first wife died somewhere between the 1871 census and the 1881 census, and then he was remarried to a Miss White. He died not long after remarrying in 1882. All three of his sons were notable gentlemen. John Paget Parker was a reverend. William Henry Parker was a Lieutenant Colonel living in Warwickshire, and Francis Parker was a well-known Worcester man, being chairman of the finance committee for the Worcester Royal infirmary and also better known for his role in schooling in Worcester. He was the voluntary school manager of St Peter's and St Martin's schools, and it was noted that during several winters he paid for all the children at St Peter's school to be fed. He was also on the rebuilding committee for St Peters Church[38].

Fig. 27: Woodside House, home to John Parker, which is still, today, a private residence.

Francis Parker was also John Parker's eldest son, so he inherited the main share of John Parker's estate upon his death including his share in Nunnery Farm[35]. Unfortunately Francis Parker died of pleurisy in 1890[38], just eight years after his father's death. The Pitchers are known to have bought Nunnery Farm off the Parkers at about this time and Francis Parker's early demise may have been a contributing factor to the estate being sold off by the Parker family.

The Pitcher family and many generations of George.

Fig. 28: The Pitcher Family outside Nunnery Farmhouse dated 1892. From the left standing – George Pitcher, Florrie, Jack, Louie and Bessie. Sitting from the left, Anne, William, Mary, Gertie, Sidney and Ernest. Reproduced with the kind permission of Robert and Beth Low, Pitcher descendants from New Zealand.

In 1848 we see the first mention of the Pitcher family at Nunnery Farm. An article in the Worcestershire Chronicle[39] places the Pitchers at Nunnery Farm in April 1848, although they were probably farming there earlier, and it mentions a sheep being stolen from George Pitcher of Nunnery Farm. The article states, *'The sheep was missed by Mr Pitcher on the day mentioned, the skin being left behind and three persons footsteps being apparent in the field. The prisoner's house was repeatedly searched afterwards and at last a piece of mutton was found in the pantry which was distinctly identified as being attached to the skin of Mr Pitchers sheep.'* The defendant claimed to have bought the sheep in the Shambles Market and was acquitted.

George Pitcher was born in Strensham in 1796. He was almost fifty by the time he took on Nunnery Farm and was an experienced farmer, having farmed previously at Woolas Hill Farm which sits just outside Great Comberton at the base of Bredon Hill[40]. It is likely that they were either already tenant farmers of William Parker's or they knew him, which was why they then moved to Worcester to farm his newly purchased estate. George Pitcher lived at Nunnery Farm with his wife Elizabeth. They had six children but by the 1851 census none of the children were living at Nunnery Farm, as they would have been old enough to either board at school (which was common amongst the middle classes) or leave home and find employment (several of the Pitcher children were recorded farming in and around Little Comberton at the time). In 1862 Elizabeth Pitcher passed away aged seventy-five, but by 1865 George Pitcher had remarried to Mary Angelina Hall who was thirty seven years his junior! In 1878 George Pitcher died and his wife Mary moved away to live with her sister at Sugarcroft Farm, Bosbury, Herefordshire[40].

George Pitcher's son William Godwin Yeend Pitcher then oversaw the running of Nunnery Farm. He did not take up residence at the farm as he lived on and managed land at Little Comberton. He installed a farm bailiff, William Hunt temporarily, until William Pitcher's son George Pitcher came of age and took on the reins of the farm, which he did in 1890[40] at the tender age of nineteen.

In 1882 John Parker died closely followed by his brother Reverend William Parker in 1884[35]. The estate was inherited by his nephews Francis Parker and William Parker Howell. At some point not long after the estate was sold, the Pitcher family finally claimed ownership of the land they'd been tenants of for almost forty years.

George Pitcher (1871–1940) married Sarah Edith Heath Bagshaw in October 1894. They had at least seven children whilst living at Nunnery Farm, the first being born in 1896[40]. In March 1901 disaster struck when George Pitcher lost his right hand in a swede cutting machine[43]. This did not stop him from continuing to run Nunnery Farm and in the same month he was elected to Pershore Rural District Council representing Whittington[44]. He continued to hold this post until his death.

George Pitcher ran Nunnery Farm mostly as a dairy farm and had an award winning herd of Shorthorn cattle on site[41]. Farms of the past were more mixed use than they are today, so often animals were kept, alongside cereal being grown and fruit being harvested. Even though George Pitcher mainly focused on cattle, we know that he also had pigs as a large swine fever outbreak was recorded at the farm in 1902[45], and various accounts of crops for sale and livestock being sold showed that Nunnery Farm was a very diverse farm.

George Pitcher was also a very keen hunter[41]. Frequent hunts are recorded as taking place across his land and through Nunnery Wood. He was a member of the Worcestershire Hunt Point to Point Committee for many years and his obituary said that despite the loss of his hand, (he made a specially adapted riding bar for use on his horse), he was still a very good horseman.

During the early 20th century parts of Nunnery Farm started to be sold off. Pressure from a booming population was starting to grow in the area for land, and at the same time a financial depression made times hard for farmers.

In 1918 a large field was sold off to the Worcestershire Corporation[15] (now Worcester City Council) by George Pitcher.

George Pitcher initially refused to sell the land and correspondence can be seen in the Worcestershire Archives in George Pitcher's strange backward slanting handwriting, probably resulting fom the loss of his hand. He protested in his letters that he didn't want the hospital buildings that were already near the site to extend into the field that was being sold. The field in question is directly adjacent to the North East side of Nunnery wood and now contains the hospital car park and main entrance.

His letters received a very curt reply from the Worcestershire Corporation stating that if they really needed the land they would simply seize it from him under compulsory purchase rules. Eventually the land was sold and was initially used as grazing for the livestock belonging to the isolation hospital, but did end up being built on long after George Pitcher's death.

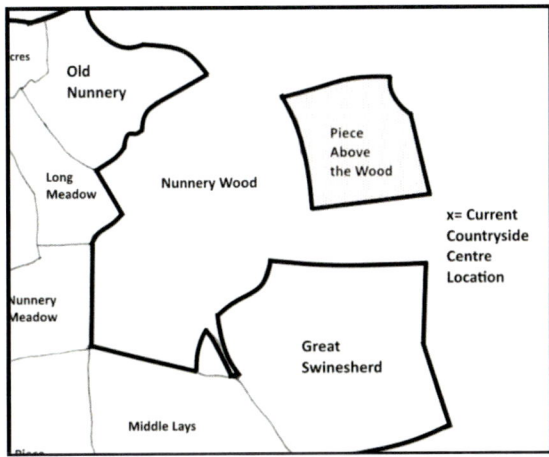

Fig. 29: Detail from Nunnery Farm Map 1850s, showing the location of the field 'Piece Above the Wood' on the top right hand side of Nunnery Wood. This was sold to the Worcester Corporation and is now part of Worcester Royal Hospital.

Fig. 30: An example of George Pitcher's backwards slanted handwriting from a letter dated 1918[15]. The strange handwriting is probably a result of his losing his right hand in a swede cutting machine in 1902.

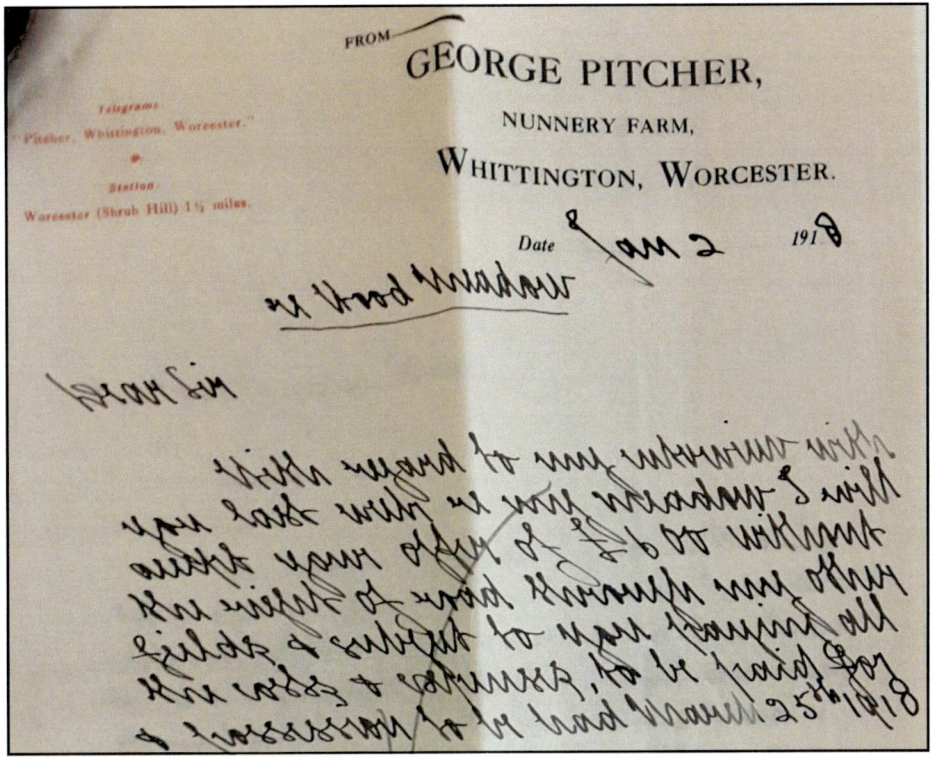

In 1922 George Pitcher caused controversy when he was fined 50 shillings for being drunk in charge of a horse and carriage[46]. He had proceeded to run over a retired Reverend! These snapshots of George Pitcher's life, gives us a faint picture of what he may have been like. Stubborn and refusing to sell land unless he got a good deal, and a rakish character with a disregard for the rules when being drunk in charge of his carriage!

By 1924 things had changed again at Nunnery Farm. George Pitcher's wife Sarah had passed away and in 1928 he remarried to a woman called Jane Rushton. By 1935 the Pitchers were disbanding Nunnery Farm and preparing for retirement. An article in the Tewkesbury Register and Agricultural Gazette[47] in 1935 had a sale notice for the auction of 650 head of poultry, eight portable poultry houses, five broody or fattening hens, three night arks, a chicken pen and five pedigree Dalmatian puppies, all being sold by a Miss Pitcher of Nunnery Farm. Although Nunnery Farm was normally labelled a cattle farm it goes to show that even in the run up to WWII farms were still very diverse.

Fig. 31 and Fig. 32: Jane Ruston the second wife of George Pitcher, and George Pitcher as a young man. Photos courtesy of Tessa Kay (Jane Rushton) and Robert and Beth Low (George Pitcher).

In the late 1930s Nunnery Farm was sold to the Worcestershire Corporation (now Worcestershire County Council). The 1939 Register, which was a census taken just at the outbreak of war, show both George Pitcher and his wife Jane living at Nunnery Cottage as Nunnery Farm was in the process of being sold[40]. George Pitcher died the following year and his wife remained at Nunnery Cottage. According to his will he also owned no 37 Spetchley Road which according to the 1939 register had Arthur Bishton and his wife Sarah living there[102]. Arthur gives his job as being a 'Horseman on Farm' and it is possible he was one of George Pitcher's employees.

Fig. 33: Nunnery cottage where George Pitcher lived after selling Nunnery Farm, which still stands on Spetchley Road.

Fig. 34: An old photo of Nunnery Cottage. Photo courtesy of Tessa Kay. No date given.

George Pitcher's funeral took place at Whittington Church. His obituary[41] describes him as being *'a bluff type of farmer with a keen sense of drollery and was regarded as good company, especially by those that care to tell and listen to stories of hunting.'* His grave can still be seen in Whittington Churchyard.

Worcestershire Corporation and Farming via Committee.

Nunnery Farm came into the hands of the Worcestershire Corporation at the outbreak of World War ll. It was purchased for £9250 which included the farm buildings and 128 acres of land[17]. The Corporation was buying up a lot of land in the area, with plans in mind for future development, but the outbreak of World War II put the brakes on these plans. This meant that the corporation now owned lots of farmland and there was enormous pressure at the time for the country to grow as much of its food as possible. Imports were being threatened and supply lines were being cut off by enemy forces. The Corporation was sitting on a large usable asset in Nunnery Farm which needed to be put back into food production. Looking in the archives, at the council minutes for the time[16] an application was made by a farmer called Mr E M Badger to take on the tenancy of Nunnery Farm for the duration of the war but this was not entertained. Instead the Worcestershire Corporation decided to manage Nunnery Farm themselves with the committee making the decisions.

A cultivation of land order was put on Nunnery Farm in 1940[16] and the committee decided to plant 48.59 acres of oats and 45.268 acres of wheat. They paid Bomford Bro £3.00 per acre to do the planting and rented a further 50 acres of land to Upper Battenhall Farm who grazed their horses there. Reading through the minutes of the committee meetings the farm was then managed by a formation of a Cultivation of Land sub-committee. In February 1941 the sub-committee approved the renting of a field to a Mr Frank Fripp who was a butcher in Sidbury. This included the use of some of the buildings in the farmyard. In July 1945 some of Mr Fripp's cattle escaped into an adjacent field and damaged beans being grown by the corporation. He was then duly evicted by the committee.

Growing food by committee was only a partial success with several crops recorded as failing and then more meetings being held to decide what to plant next. Once the war was over the farming operation at Nunnery Farm was disbanded. An advert in the Tewksbury Register and Agricultural Gazette[48] in 1948 was advertising the sale of *'40 Fordson Tractors and a capital collection of agricultural implements.'* It was likely that Nunnery Farm wasn't the only bit of land farmed by the

Fig. 35: The back view of Nunnery Farm prior to demolition in 1951. Photograph courtesy of Jim Bishop.

Worcestershire Corporation during the war and the Nunnery Farm buildings were probably used as storage for the corporation's agricultural kit hence having so many tractors for sale.

After this point Nunnery Farm stood empty and decaying and it was demolished in 1958 after falling into an increasingly dilapidated state. The surrounding farmland then became Nunnery Wood School and the college, County Hall, grounds and lakes with Nunnery Wood becoming half of Worcester Woods Country Park.

Fig. 36: Jim Bishop on a tractor at Nunnery Farm in 1951. Photo courtesy of Jim Bishop.

Fig. 37: Two young boys in a barn at Nunnery Farm in 1951. Photo courtesy of Jim Bishop.

Fig. 38: A fire engine on Nunnery Farm having attended a farm fire in one of the fields. 1951. Photo Courtesy of Jim Bishop.

Nunnery Wood.

Nunnery Wood originally would have been part of The Forest of Feckenham[4]. It is thought, although we are not certain, that Nunnery Wood was owned by the nuns at Whitstones who were the order of White Ladies Nunnery[101]. There are several orders of Whitstones Nuns around the country so we are making a presumption that Nunnery Wood was owned by the local order. Kingsbury (1984)[101] states that; St Wulstans Hospital may have also owned the wood for a time in the pre-Tudor period. We know that Nunnery Wood hasn't always been continuously wooded, as ridge and furrow earthworks are still clearly visible within the Wood (ridge and furrow is a medieval type of field ploughing system which leaves a distinctive undulating pattern on the ground). The presence of ridge and furrow earthworks show Nunnery Wood went through a previous period of usage as farmland before reverting back to woodland. This could have occurred in the 1300s when the Black Death wiped out a lot of the farming population, meaning that there weren't enough people left to work the land, causing a lot of farmland to revert back to being wooded.

The White Ladies Nunnery was set up in 1255 as a Benedictine order and the Nunnery was situated at Whistones in Claines[4]. Nunnery Wood and its neighbour Nunnery Farm were, we think, both owned by the Nunnery and would have provided food and timber to meet the needs of the nuns. It is thought Nunnery Wood remained in the hands of White Ladies until 1536[4] when the Reformation took place. This led to King Henry VIII breaking with the Catholic Church and as a result he confiscated a lot of their land and assets. Nunnery Wood was given to Christchurch College in Oxford in 1546[101] after the White Ladies Nunnery was dissolved. Christchurch College still own part of Nunnery Wood to this day.

It is thought that Nunnery Wood derives its name from this period of ownership by the White Ladies Nuns. According to Kingsbury (1984)[101] the name of Nunnery Wood was far more recent than the naming of the neighbouring Perry Wood which we think was first documented from the late Anglo Saxon period with better documentary evidence from 1370. Nunnery Wood is thought to have got its name as late as the second half of the 1700s. Kingsbury (1984)[101] did state that the name Nunnery Wood may have been in use in the middle ages and then fallen out of use for a while before coming back again in the 1700s but without more documentary evidence we can't be sure.

Nunnery Wood was sublet by Christchurch College to various tenants including some of the local farms. At times it was included in maps as part of the Ronkswood Farm estate[94], along with

Nunnery Farmland, and this seemed to be the case until at least the early 1800s when the wood then appeared to be managed by various tenants. Then it appears in the mid 1800s as being part of the Nunnery Farm estate but was not included with Ronkswood Farm Estate.

The earliest map of Nunnery Wood I can find is a 1751 map[94] which shows Nunnery Wood and Ronkswood Farm plus Perry Wood together (Nunnery and Perry Wood were often parcelled in together and managed by the same tenants). The map gave the owners as being Richard Hawkins and William Russell, although it is likely they were the lessees as Nunnery Wood and Perry Wood was in the hands of Christchurch College at the time. On this map the wood can be seen as being roughly a similar shape to the present day shape with a bit extra at the northern tip. Kingsbury (1984)[101] stated that in 1809 William Oldnall Russell wanted to take Nunnery Wood with a mind to stocking it up (removing the trees and their roots to make farmland). This could have been the son of William Russell. This plan to remove some of the woodland did not come to fruition as John Hill was given as having the lease in 1814.

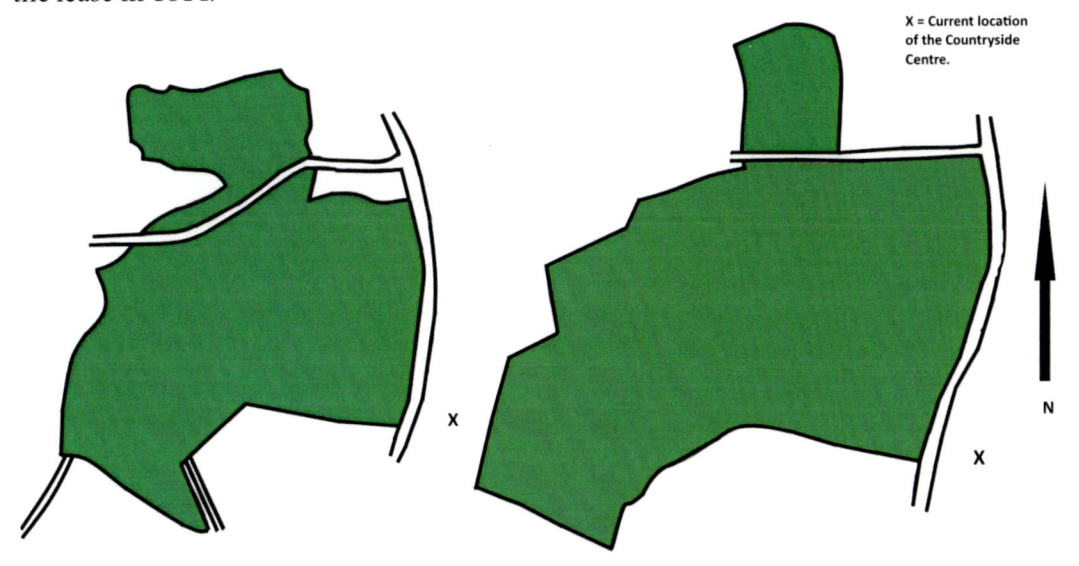

Fig. 39: The Changing outline of Nunnery Wood. Old maps show Nunnery Wood 1814 on the left. After 1838 this changed and it became the shape it still is today with the 1938 outline on the right showing its modern outline.

By 1814 Nunnery Wood was being sold as part of Nunnery Farm and Ronkswood Estate. The estate was being auctioned off in lots. Although still owned by Christchurch College the lease was presumably being auctioned off with the existing tenants being sub-lessees. The Auction notice gives John Hill as being a leaseholder of the wood. Nunnery Wood was given as Lot 13, *'An estate called Nunnery Wood consisting of valuable coppice land, principally oak coppice and also of a small piece (not quite an acre) of valuable meadow or pasture land called the Wood Pleck, the said Nunnery Wood being in the occupation of Mr John Hill whose lease expires on 1st Nov 1823 and the Wood Pleck being in the occupation of Mr Benjamin Fieldhouse whose lease expires 1st Nov 1816.'*[49]

By 1820 John Knapp had purchased the lease for Nunnery Wood whilst Nunnery Farm as an estate remained unsold. Several attempts were made to sell Nunnery Farm in 1824 and 1832 and 1836, when the farm was thought to have eventually passed into the hands of the Parker Family. We think at this point the lease of Nunnery Wood could have also become property of the Parker family. Various documents held within the Worcestershire Archives[12] show that Nunnery Wood was certainly in the hands of Rev William Parker and his brother John Parker Esq by 1857, with rents on Nunnery Wood and income from bark being sold to someone called 'Broadfield' for tanning and poles being sold to someone called 'Hayes'. As George Pitcher was regularly placing adverts looking for labourers with knowledge of coppicing and tanning, it is very likely he was overseeing the management of Nunnery Wood as part of Nunnery Farm, on behalf of the Parker Brothers.

Tanning was an important part of the produce from Nunnery Wood, and Kingsbury (1984)[101] mentions in 1847 the price of bark for tanning went down due to imports of cheap bark from Europe and the invention of chemicals that could be used in the tanning process, leading to less use of bark. The rental prices had already risen steeply over the preceding years with yearly rental being valued at £54.1.0 in 1813, but by 1827 it had risen to a yearly rental of £70. As the price of wood products hadn't risen accordingly, this resulted in disputes between the lessee and Christchurch College over the high rent paid for Nunnery Wood.

This coincides with proposals which were made to break up Nunnery Wood. A plan[101] was produced in 1847 with the wood split into four roughly equal pieces. Each piece was proposed to be 'stocked up' which meant clearing the wood with a mind to converting it into farmland. As cereal prices were at an all-time high and woodland produce was decreasing in value this approach made sound economic sense. The wood was still producing a lot of timber at this time and was managed by a woodsman known as 'Bradley'. This was probably when the north western tip of Nunnery Wood which now forms part of Newtown Green was removed. Fortunately the plan to stock up the rest of Nunnery Wood was not followed through.

In the 1880s there were two stories in the local papers about theft from Nunnery Wood. An article in 1880 in the Worcestershire Chronicle[50] talks about two men being charged with damaging underwood in Nunnery Wood. It states *'William Ravenscroft overseer of the ground for Mr Parker, Red Hill, said he saw the defendants cutting wood with an axe and a knife in Nunnery Wood. They both ran away when they saw him, leaving 15 sticks behind them.'*

William Ravenscroft caught both of the men who asked to be forgiven but they ended up in court instead and being fined five shillings each. Three years later in 1883[51] an article appeared in the Worcester Journal[51] *'Caught at last. Henry Whitlock of no fixed residence was charged with setting snares on 6th Dec 1879 in the Nunnery Wood. He, not being the holder of a game certificate and further with unlawfully having a rabbit in his possession on Jan 1st 1883.'*

Henry Whitlock ended up being fined ten shillings for both offences. Theft of Game, crops and woodland produce such as poles and timber were common, with gamekeepers and woodsmen constantly trying to catch the culprits and keep them out of the wood.

It is thought that a lot of active woodland management had stopped by the 1930s when wood prices were being depressed by cheap European imports. Most woods fell out of cultivation by this point and Nunnery Wood seems to be no exception. This and housing pressure on the surrounding land put Nunnery Wood under strain.

By 1918 the scenery directly around Nunnery Wood was beginning to change. Land was being brought up around the wood by the Worcestershire Corporation (now Worcester City Council).The pressure on land continued until finally in 1940 Nunnery Farm was sold to the Worcestershire Corporation. Minutes from council meetings held in the 1930s and 1940s[17] show repeated attempts by the Worcestershire Corporation to buy Nunnery Wood from Christchurch College. This started in Dec 1937. At some point part of Nunnery Wood was purchased from Christchurch and this may have been a compulsory purchase as part of the hospital expansion. As a result the northern part of Nunnery Wood now belongs to Worcester City Council, having been passed onto them by the health authority in the 1970s.

In 1942 Worcestershire Corporation was again trying to purchase Nunnery Wood from Christchurch College who again refused to sell it to them. At the same time Christchurch College was selling the timber, as standing timber from the whole wood. Minutes from Council meetings at this time show that Worcestershire Corporation brought up 9.5 acres of timber from Nunnery Wood at the cost of £3 per acre in 1945. As this was towards the end of WWII it is likely that resources were scarce at this time hence the council buying up timber stocks. In 1946 the whole of Nunnery Wood apart from the boundary trees were clear felled. Aerial photos from the time show the wood bare, with a thick boundary edge still in place. After the wood was clear felled it was then left to regrow. That is why all the old trees can be seen around the edge of the wood and the rest of the trees are the same age within the wood.

In October 1979 Christchurch College finally leased Nunnery Wood to Hereford and Worcester County Council. This was the beginning of Worcester Woods Country Park. Perry Wood was also acquired plus the land where the Countryside Centre is now situated. In 1987 to celebrate the opening of the new Countryside Centre, Nunnery Wood was designated a Local Nature Reserve and has since been managed for wildlife and recreation as part of Worcester Woods Country Park

Newtown Grange

Newtown Grange was a large red bricked 19th Century farmhouse with surrounding buildings based just off Newtown Road near the Worcestershire Royal Hospital site. The farm was demolished in the 1970s, but the pine trees that surrounded it can still be seen on the hospital site opposite the entrance to Aconbury Close.

Fig. 40: The pine trees that used to surround Newtown Grange, which can still be seen as part of the hospital complex. View from Newtown Road.

The northern tip of the farm originally stretched across the opposite side of Newtown road encompassing the area that is now Leopold Rise, Oaklands, The Heights, Aconbury Close and Aconbury Orchard. The Southern side of Newtown Grange was a long rectangular spur that came out past Newtown Grange farmhouse and encompassed the current Worcester Woods Country Park Countryside Centre, the main field with the picnic area, car park and St Richards Hospice.

According to Hopper (2011)[2] Newtown Grange originally formed part of the Manor of Lyppard which belonged to a monastery in Worcester in the 15th Century. The inclusion of 'Grange' in its name denotes that it was an outlying farm of a monastery.

The earliest reference I can find to Newtown Grange is a mention in a book called 'A history of Worcestershire Agriculture and Rural Revolution'[87] published in 1939. There's a paragraph referring to the sale of the estate in 1766. It was 100 acres at the time, and the yearly rent was £69.

The book quotes from the advert selling the estate and describes the estate as *'Very eligible to any gentleman of an easy fortune or tradesman retiring from business who might like to amuse himself in the occupation of a commodious farm.'*

The next reference we can find to Newtown Grange is in a 1790 map of the Nunnery Farm

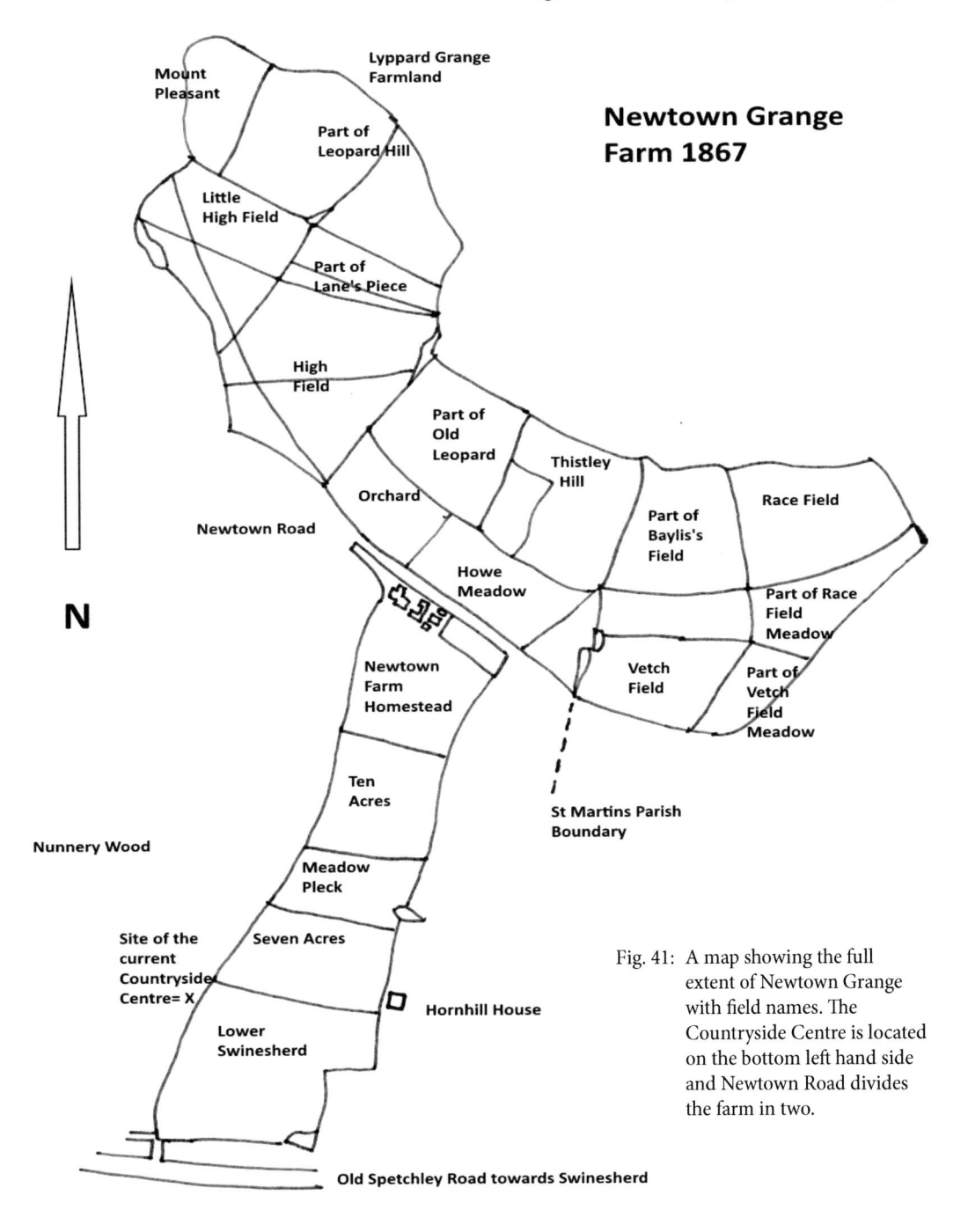

Fig. 41: A map showing the full extent of Newtown Grange with field names. The Countryside Centre is located on the bottom left hand side and Newtown Road divides the farm in two.

Estate[7]. This shows Newtown Grange farmhouse above Nunnery Wood. The drawing was quite simplistic and may or may not have been based on a building that predated the more modern red brick farmhouse.

In the early 1800s Newtown Grange was farmed by John Green. He was named on an 1834 map of Nunnery Farm as an adjacent landowner of Newtown Grange[88], and was also named on an 1838 map of Swinesherd Farm as an adjacent landowner[9].

According to Berrows Journal John Green died on 15th March 1852 aged eighty-one. His wife was found dead in her bed[54] by one of her servants, a month later on 25th April 1852. A plaque commemorating him and his two wives can be seen in the old St Martins Church at the Cornmarket.

According to Hopper 2011[2] John Green went into production as an implement maker and supplier. He regularly invented his own farming implements which he exhibited at various agricultural shows. This was continued by his son, who was also called John Green when he inherited the running of the farm after his father's death in 1852. An article in a newspaper in 1864 stated *'Mr John Green of Newtown Farm near Worcester exhibited a cultivating and couch destroying plough which it is alleged will plough a furrow ten or twelve inches wide, from three to nine inches deep.'* The article then goes on to talk about other inventions of John Green including *'A set of flexible harrows, a pair of three beam harrows and a clod crusher which consisted of a number of teeth or cutting projections cast upon three corner bars which together pulverise the soil effectively.'*[52]

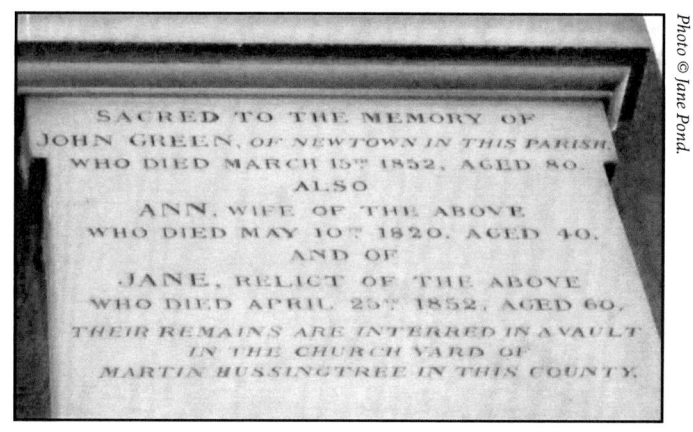

Fig. 42: Plaque in St Martins Church, Cornmarket in memory of John Green and his two wives Ann and Jane.

These machines were exhibited at the Royal Agricultural Society show in Newcastle Upon Tyne in July 1864. The previous year John Green had sent a patent cultivating couch destroying plough and a patent cultivator and couch extirpator to the Royal Agricultural Society to be viewed.[53] Farming in the mid 1800s was a time of invention and expansion. At the time of John Green's inventions, farming was going through a boom period and farmers would have had the money to invest in new machinery thus opening up markets and leading to innovation.

John Green left the farm when Newtown Grange was sold in 1867[10].

The sale particulars for the farm lists *'A cow house to tie up eighteen cows with foddering walks, root and chaff house, calves pen, hack and cart stables. Superior piggeries particularly well arranged with wood wash reservoir and tank.'*

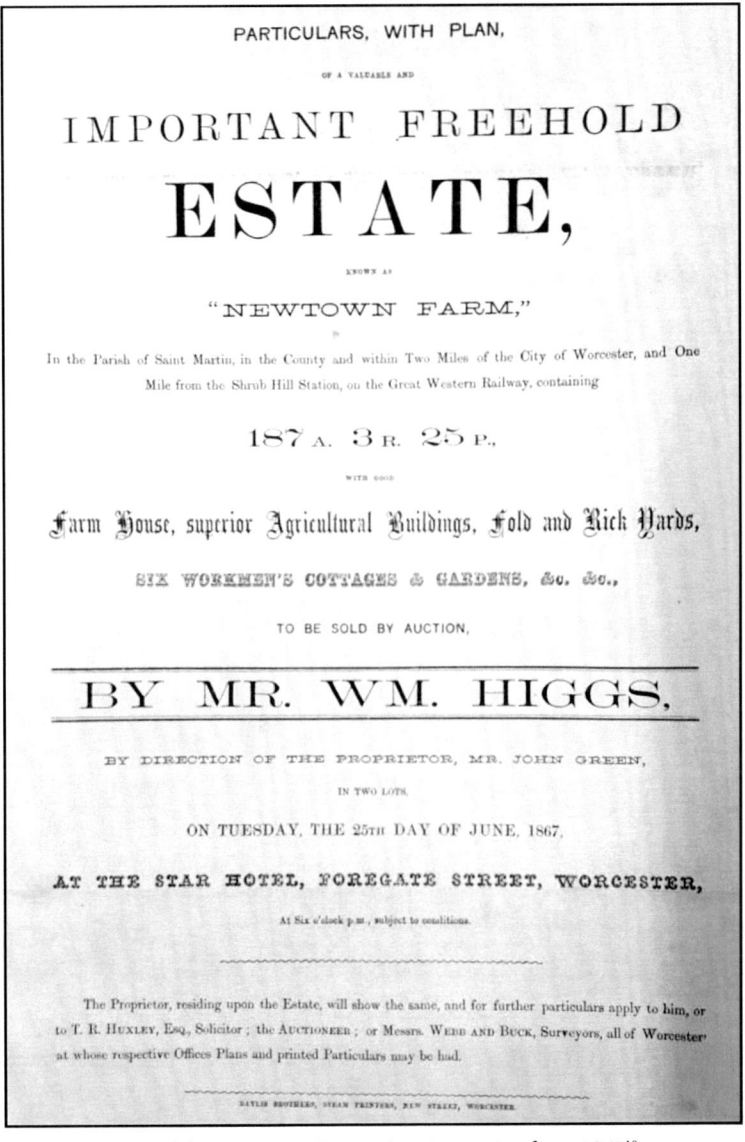

Fig. 43: A copy of the Newtown Grange Auction notice from 1867[10].

The sale particulars also list, *'A very good stone cider mill and spacious mill house. The estate lies well for game, being nearly surrounded by the lands and preserves of Robert Berkeley and John Parker Esq.'* There were several orchards at Newtown Grange, with cider and perry making an important part of the farm.

We know from looking at the census that after John Green left Newtown Grange he then went onto manage Brickbarns farm at Broadheath where he met and later married his housekeeper.

By 1871 John Lane was living and farming at Newtown Grange with his wife Sarah and two young children. They did not stay at the farm long so were most likely tenants rather than the owners. By 1881 they were farming at Stonebow Farm and then they moved on to farm at Upper Wolverton Farm near Spetchley.

In the 1881 census Thomas Smith was listed as living at Newtown Grange with his wife Charlotte Alice. He had previously married Charlotte Alice in 1878 and was listed in the Worcestershire Chronicle[55] as inhabiting Newtown Grange at the time of the marriage. Charlotte Alice Smith's maiden name was Holland and she was the second eldest daughter of notable Worcester man Walter Holland (1833–1888). Walter Holland ran the Vulcan Iron works in Worcester under a company called McKenzie and Holland. The business was international and did a lot of trade in Australia. He was elected councillor for Claines in

1862 until 1881, and was elected mayor of Worcester in 1878 and again in 1886[56]. His portrait can be seen still hanging in the Guildhall at Worcester. Walter Holland was also a rectors' warden for eighteen years at St Martins Church in Cornmarket.

Walter Holland died in 1888. The Worcestershire Chronicle[56] did a full page and at that time both Thomas Smith and his wife Charlotte were listed as being principle mourners at his funeral. After Walter Holland's death the Smiths left Newtown Grange and I have been unable to trace them. My best guess is that they may have emigrated to somewhere like Australia, where they may have taken on a role in running the family business abroad after Walter Holland had died.

Fig. 44: A picture of Walter Holland's portrait which can be seen hanging in the Guildhall in Worcester.

John Herbert 'Bertie' Somer.

The fate of the Smiths may remain a mystery, but in 1891 Newtown Grange was occupied by John Herbert Somer, who, at the tender age of twenty-two, was stated as being head of the house where he lived with three younger sisters, his father John and mother Jane. According to the census the family had moved up from Cornwall, where they'd previously been farming land. In 1894 some of the Newtown Grange land was sold off and turned into an isolation hospital. By 1900 John Herbert Somer had joined the Imperial Yeomanry and gone off to war leaving his father John Somer in charge of the farm[57]. By 1901 Newtown Grange was empty. John Somer had moved out and presumably his son John Herbert was still in the army, as no one had replaced the family at the farm.

According to the census, the Somers then moved to Wadborough where John Herbert's father, John Somer, was still farming with his wife Jane. John Herbert was still not listed but his brother William was living there, despite his occupation listed as being a trooper in the Imperial Yeomanry. By 1911 the family were still at Wadborough and John Herbert was back with the family and working on the farm again. Interestingly on the 1911 census for Newtown Grange John Herbert Somer is listed as being head of the family or separate occupier for Newtown

Grange despite not being resident there. This probably meant he still owned and oversaw the running of the farm despite still living in Wadborough. The house next door was listed as having George Hitchins as resident who was a farm labourer at Newtown Grange for many years.

At some point after 1911 John Herbert returned with one of his sisters to Newtown Grange and continued to farm at the Grange. Certainly by 1926 he had returned to Newtown Grange, as he was living there with his mother when she died (Newtown Grange is mentioned in her probate). He is mentioned in tithe records in 1936 as being resident and farmer there. The 1939 England and Wales Register also lists him as living at Newtown Grange with his sister Mary. John Herbert Somer remained there until his death in 1953.

John Herbert Somer is remembered fondly by one local man, Maurice Jones, who lived in the area as a child and remembers childhood days spent in around Newtown Grange. He said John Herbert was known by everyone as Bertie Somer or Mr Somer as the children had to call him! He was known as a colourful local character with a great big handlebar moustache who drove around in a blue open-topped car. Bertie Somer used to deliver milk to the local cottages in a horse and trap. He had milk churns on the back and he measured the milk out into a jug which was poured into bottles that people brought with them from their houses.

Maurice Jones also tells the story of a man called Charlie who lived in one of the barns at Newtown Grange. Charlie was homeless, having served in the First World War and suffering ever since. Maurice said he was a very polite well educated man. Charlie never worked as he was unable to, but Bertie Somer let him live in the barn anyway as he had nowhere else to go.

Maurice's father Arthur Jones was great friends with one of Bertie Somer's farm labourers, George Hitchins. In later years George Hitchins lived with his wife Elsie in a brick house right down the end of Newtown Road towards Spetchley. Some of the bricks that formed the outside toilet can still be seen by the roadside (Fig. 45). George regularly used to ride on horseback with Arthur Jones on a Sunday down to the Pear Tree Inn at Smite, and apparently after too much perry and cider they would usually have to rely upon the horses to bring them back!

Maurice Jones also remembers the gathering of the harvest at Aconbury Orchard. Every autumn the apples and pears would be picked and brought back to Newtown Grange where they were pressed and turned into cider and perry. It sounded like a social event with locals helping out probably getting paid for their labour with free cider!

John Herbert Somer, or Bertie as he was

Fig. 45: The only remnants of the house belonging to George Hitchins- a small outhouse which can still be seen on the side of Newtown Road.

known, died on 21st June 1953, and at this point the farm was sold to Albert Newell or Bert Newell as he was known. Bert Newell farmed Trotshill farm and when he took on Newtown Grange he installed George Hitchins to run the farm for him. George Hitchins continued to run the farm until he retired (by then he was in his eighties) in the early 1970s. After George retired Bert Newell sold the farm and Newtown Grange was demolished and turned into a mortuary for the hospital and the rest of the land was sold off, becoming part of the hospital grounds, housing, and part of Worcester Woods Country Park.

Swinesherd Farm and the Watson Family

Swinesherd Farm is the outlier of the four farms that formed Worcester Woods Country Park, with just the Northern tip covering part of the land of what now forms the Country Park. It is also the only one of the four farms from this era where some of the farm buildings still survive. Swinesherd Farm was situated on the old Spetchley Road. The farm consisted of a courtyard of farm buildings including the main farmhouse and a steam powered cornmill. The cornmill and some farm buildings still survive as private housing and can be seen at Swinesherd just over the motorway bridge in a cul-de-sac off the A44.

Fig. 46: The Cornmill was originally part of Swinesherd Farm and is now a private residence.

The farm was owned by the Berkeley Family who own Spetchley Park and many other surrounding farms. It was let out to tenant farmers. According to Hopper (2011)[2] Swinesherd was farmed by John Hartwright (1753-1837) for most of his life with the Watson Family taking over and running the farm from the 1830s until the 1930s.

Swinesherd Farm was a large farm of about 250 acres (about 100 hectares). It surrounded Hornhill Farm, and at times Hornhill Farm and Hornhill house were sublet by the tenants of Swinesherd Farm and the two were run together. Swinesherd Farm covered the South Eastern part of Worcester Woods Country Park and then spread out along where the M5 is currently situated.

I am not sure when the Watson Family first moved to Swinesherd Farm but there are certainly references to them being resident there in the late 1830s. The farm itself was probably built in the mid 1700s although an exact build date couldn't be found.

John Watson was the first Watson to farm at Swinesherd. John Watson was born in Ansley,

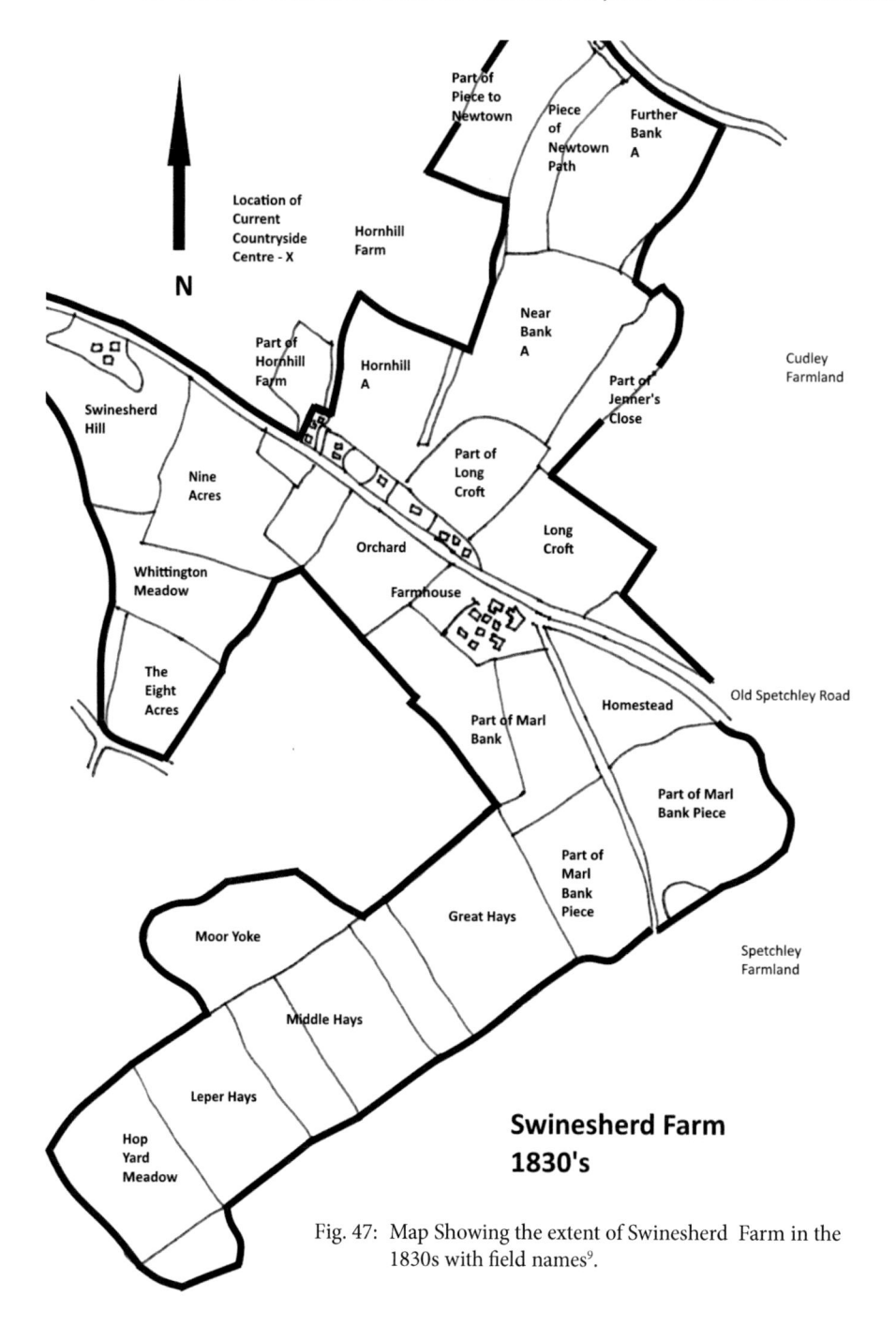

Fig. 47: Map Showing the extent of Swinesherd Farm in the 1830s with field names[9].

Warwickshire in 1789. He married his wife Ann Cash in Nuneaton, Warwickshire in 1816 and they then had several children, Thomas being their eldest, plus Edwin, then Mary Ann, Arthur, William, Sarah Jane, Elizabeth and Henry. Mary Ann was born at Nuneaton in 1823 whereas Arthur was born in St Johns Worcester in 1825. All subsequent siblings were born in St Johns with William the youngest being born in 1831[58]. As most children were born at home at that time it seems likely they moved to Swinesherd after 1831. An 1838 estate map[9] gives John Watson as being tenant of Swinesherd Farm, but according to sales particulars[11] for the sale of Nunnery Farm in 1836, John Watson was also tenant there. I am unsure as to whether he was farming both together but by 1838 Thomas Porter was being listed as tenant for Nunnery Farm and John Watson had moved on to farm at Swinesherd.

An interesting side note. Whilst researching John Watson at Swinesherd I came across an Edward Watson farming at Spetchley Farm in the late 1830s. Further research revealed that Edward was John Watson's brother. They were born just one year apart and both lived in Warwickshire before deciding to move to Worcestershire to farm Swinesherd and Spetchley. Edward Watson's wife Maria and six sons all lived on the farm (a seventh son lived in Warwickshire). The family became beset by tragedy when the eldest son (also called Edward) died in 1842 aged eighteen. A year later Maria died in January 1843 and was buried in Whittington Churchyard, then in 1845 Edward died in Cookshill Warwickshire, having left the farm, and was buried at Astley. A notice in the Worcester Journal Jan 1846[59] had all of Mr Watsons farming goods and effects being sold off at Spetchley Farm to make way for new tenants.

During this time John Watson was also suffering his own misfortune at Swinesherd Farm. In 1840 disaster struck when John Watson was run over by a horse drawn hay making machine in one of the fields at Swinesherd. The account given in the Worcester Journal runs as follows[60], *'On Friday last Mr John Watson of Swinesherd in the county was leading a young horse attached to a hay making machine in one of his fields when the animal suddenly became restive and set off at full speed. Mr Watson was knocked down and it was supposed that the wheel went over his leg as it was found to be fractured in two places. As the cylinder revolved the spikes caught hold of Mr Watsons clothes from behind and he was tossed completely over the machine. We are glad to learn the Mr Watson is going on very favourably.'*

Industrial accidents were very common especially on farms, but despite his injuries John Watson continued to farm at Swinesherd before retiring in the 1840s. He obviously felt fortunate to survive his accident as he appears in the Worcester Journal in 1842[61] giving a generous donation to rebuilding Whittington Church. The current church was said to be in a very decayed state and too small for the growing parish, so a complete rebuild was proposed which happened in the mid 1840s. A lot of local people are listed as donating towards the new church, and from a visit to the church it can be seen that there are many members of the Watson family buried there. Once retired John Watson and his wife moved in with his eldest son, Thomas, who farmed near Shrawley where they appear on the 1851 census. He died at Shrawley in 1856.

Meanwhile, his second eldest son Edwin Watson took over the running of Swinesherd Farm. Information from the archivist at Spetchley Park states that 'In 1851 there was an agreement drawn up between Robert Berkeley and Edwin Watson dated 2nd June 1851 in which Edwin was granted permission to erect a building near the homestead at Swinesherd to be used as a cornmill and worked by steam power.' Part of the agreement also stated that he had to take the equipment with him when he left the farm. At this point milling became an important part of the Swinesherd Farm operation. People from the surrounding area would have brought their corn to Swinesherd to be milled.

The census for 1851 states that, Edwin was a *'farmer of 263 acres and nine labourers.'* This census provides us with a very interesting detail about the Watson family. Edwin aged thirty-one was now head of the farm but still had five of his younger siblings living with him. His sister Sarah Jane acted as house keeper. Three of his siblings, Arthur, Elizabeth and William were stated as being blind. It is not known what became of William, but in the 1861 census Arthur and Mary Ann are still living with Edwin at Swinesherd and Arthur is stated as being blind from birth. Elizabeth ended up in Shrawley living with her brother Thomas at East Grove Farm. Thomas died in 1865 but his sister Sarah Jane then moved into the farmhouse to become its house keeper and looked after her blind sister Elizabeth. Arthur stayed at Swinesherd Farm and worked with his brother until at least 1871. By the 1881 census he was living with his brother Joseph in Yardley, Warwickshire and unable to work. He died in 1882.

Back at Swinesherd Farm, Edwin Watson was married in 1853 to Mary Ann Ridgeway[58]. Sadly the marriage only lasted to 1864 when Mary Ann died after a long illness. They hadn't had any children during the marriage and two years later Edwin remarried again, this time to Hanna Morris in 1864. They went on to have three children, Mary, John and Edwin.

Whilst Edwin Watson was running Swinesherd Farm a theme that kept coming up when researching him was his love of steam. After applying to install a steam powered cornmill in 1851, he went on to form a steam plough company with Mr Green of Newtown Farm and Mr Dudfield of Sneachhill Farm. An item such as a steam engine drawn plough would have been a very expensive thing to buy, so the easiest way for farmers to afford running one was to pool their resources and then share use of the item.

An article in the Worcester Chronicle 1861[62] stated: *'It will be remembered that some time ago great efforts were made of Mr Green of Newtown near this city for the formation of a steam plough company with a view of introducing that important agricultural implement into the neighbourhood. The proposition failed from want of cordial support on the part of the agriculturalists. Two of Mr Green's neighbours however, Mr Watson of Swinesherd and Mr Dudfield of Sneachhill impressed with the importance of introducing the new implement into agriculture have since joined Mr Green and purchased with their joint purse one of the latest improved steam ploughs – Fowlers patent, manufactured by Kitson and co of Leeds, which was at work on Thursday and Friday on stiff wheat stubble in the farm of Mr Watson.'*

Fig. 48: A 1916 Fowlers steam engine and plough in action at the Welland Steam Fayre.

The article went onto to talk about the spectacle of the steam plough arriving by train into Spetchley Station and then being driven down Spetchley Road with crowds of onlookers lining the streets to catch a glimpse of this strange new mechanical beast. It was said the steam plough could plough an acre an hour. It took at least four men to work the plough and initially cost £825 to buy, a small fortune in the 1860s! A year later, Edwin Watson was in the Berrow's Worcester Journal 1862[89]. This time he was in a row with the operators of the toll on London Road who were trying to charge him for not paying a toll for driving the steam plough down London road. Edwin was refusing to pay the toll as he said the plough was exempt under the General Turnpike Act as it was used for agricultural purposes. The court found in favour of the London Road toll and Edwin Watson had to pay for the plough to use the toll gate.

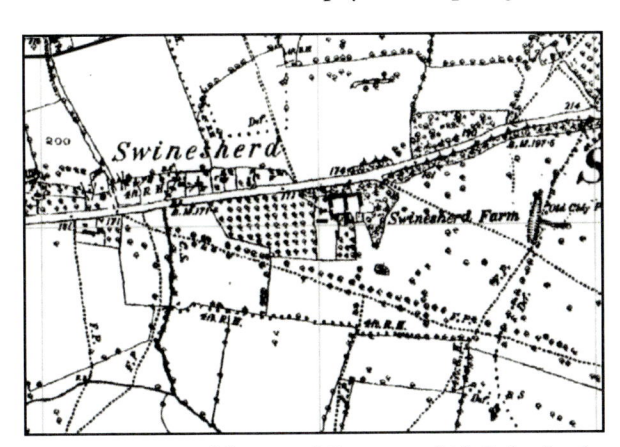

Fig. 49: A section of the 1890 O.S map on which Swinesherd Orchard is clearly shown as straight regimented trees in a field next to the farm. Another orchard can be seen in the top right hand corner.

Swinesherd Farm under Edwin Watson was a mixed farm with arable crops and cattle. Edwin owned an award winning herd of shorthorn cows and he crops up in regular newspaper articles being awarded prizes at agricultural shows for his cattle. A notice appeared in the Bells Weekly Messenger[63] in 1868 which was advertising for a farm bailiff for Swinesherd Mill. The advert stated the candidate *'must understand fruit and hops'*. The farm would have had orchards as part of its crops and these can be seen near the farm on the 1890 Ordnance

Survey Map. Orchards can be clearly seen marked on old OS maps as lines of regimented trees, rather than scattered trees which denote woodland.

By 1880 Edwin was selling off his assets and leaving the farm. An auction notice appeared in the Worcester Journal in 1880[64] selling (as instructed by Mr E Watson) *'The breeding portion of his valuable herd of Shorthorn cattle comprising of about forty head.'* Farm implements, lambs and working horses were also included in the auction.

A sale of Hornhill Farm notice in 1884[22] gives Edwin Watson as being tenant there, so he possibly downsized, to run a smallholding as he got older. His two sons John (born 1870) and Edwin (born 1869) were still too young to run Swinesherd Farm, so for a time new tenants ran the farm. John H Cartidge was listed in the Michaelmas rent as being tenant in 1883. Stephen Bennett took over Michaelmas 1885 and stayed until 1905 when the farm was briefly tenanted by A W Bomford before going back to Edwin and John Watson[65]. During this time the Watson brothers were still involved in Swinesherd. The 1891 census gives the two brothers and their sister Mary as living in Redhill. Both brothers had their occupation down as being millers and were very likely involved in running the mill at Swinesherd. Their father Edwin Watson died in February 1891 and was buried at Whittington. Mary their sister died in 1893.

The Watson brothers were certainly active members of the local community. In 1899 both were members of Whittington Parish Council[66] with Edwin Watson being voted in as chairman and his brother John being on the council along with George Pitcher who farmed Nunnery Farm. We also know from a plaque in All Saints Church at Spetchley that John Watson was a churchwarden there for nearly fifty one years.

In 1900 an article in the Worcestershire Chronicle[67] describes a farm fire at Aston Hall, White Ladies Aston where *'Messrs Watson Brothers of Swinesherd'* had a threshing machine and straw trusser destroyed whilst they were working there. As farm machinery was still very expensive at the turn of the century, other farmers would have paid for farmers with machinery to come and help harvest crops and prepare soil. The Watson brothers obviously made a living doing just this. By 1901 both brothers were living back at Swinesherd in Avenue Lodge with Edwin's wife Ann. Their occupations were both given as 'corn miller and threshing machine proprietor.' So the threshing machine must have been replaced after the fire and was an important part of their income.

By 1908 both men were married. Edwin had married Ann in 1899 and John had married

Fig. 50: Picture of the plaque in All Saints Church at Spetchley dedicated to John Watson.

Marian in 1903. Both brothers were still living in and around Swinesherd Farm when a huge tragedy befell the family. Both Edwin's wife Anne and John's wife, Marian were pregnant. They gave birth within ten days of each other with Ann having her third child Charles Edwin Watson on June 25th 1908. Maria then had her first child, a boy named John on 5th July 1908. A headstone can be seen in All Saints Churchyard at Spetchley where Maria died on 22nd July 1908 and her baby died 23rd July 1908. Sadly Ann's baby Charles Edwin Watson also died on 12th May 1909. Although it was common to lose children, the closeness of the families must have made this an unimaginably painful tragedy to bear.

In 1911, the census gave Edwin Watson as living at Avenue Lodge with his wife Ann and their two remaining children, Mary and Emily Louisa. Edwin's profession is listed as Corn miller and farmer, tying in with the fact that they'd taken Swinesherd Farm back in hand.

Fig. 51: Gravestone of Marian Watson in All Saints Churchyard, Spetchley.

Meanwhile, Edwin's brother John was living back at Swinesherd Farm on his own with just one servant, and his occupation is now given solely as being a farmer.

John Watson did remarry in 1922 to Dorothy Frances Thomas and I believe they had a daughter named Elizabeth. In 1930 Edwin Watson died and is buried with his wife Ann (who died in 1944) at Whittington Church. In 1931 John gave up the tenancy of Swinesherd Farm. At the time he was Farming at Home Farm, Spetchley (Spetchley Farm) where he continued to live. He probably found two farms too much to run without his brother. A sale notice in the Tewkesbury Register and Agricultural Gazette[68] announced the sale by *'The trustees of the late E Watson and Mr John Watson of corn mill machinery including a Hornsby 18 BHP oil engine, steel shafting and fast and loose pulley wheels, plus iron force pump, three pairs of french buhr and Derbyshire peak millstones with casings and driving gear. Blackmores, flour dresses, corn screener, smutter and corn kibblers.'*

John Watson continued to live at Home Farm, Spetchley at least until 1939 when he is listed on the 1939 England and Wales register as living there as a farmer with his wife Dorothy. In the same register Edwin Watson's wife, Ann, still lived at Avenue Lodge with her daughter, Emily Louisa, caring for her, her status was given in the register as being incapacitated. Looking through the 1939 register I could find no mention of anyone farming at Swinesherd Mill, so it appears to have been rented as a private residence probably with the fields being let to nearby farmers. There was also no evidence of the cornmill still being in use, so it seems likely that when the milling tools were sold off in 1931, that was the end of the use of the cornmill. The archivist at Spetchley Park did say that during this period times were very hard financially for farmers and there were a lot of cases of tenants asking for rent reductions and giving up farms. This would then tie in with the farmhouse being let out as a private residence.

John Watson passed away on 24th Jan 1952 and his wife Dorothy in 1976. By then she was living in Droitwich but both are buried in All Saints graveyard at Spetchley. Swinesherd Mill Farm meanwhile was broken up, with a large part of it forming the first phase of the M5 in 1962. The rest was sold off to various organisations, some being used for private housing and part forming Worcester Woods Country Park.

Fig. 52: An old photo of the building of the new Spetchley Road motorway bridge in 1960 with the Swinesherd Farm buildings in the background[90]. Credit B Buckle.

Farming life in the Victorian and Edwardian era

Life on the farms.

From various sources of information you can get a feel for what life was like living and working on these farms in the past. Out of the four farms that made up Worcester Woods Country Park three of them were medium to large sized farms for the area, with Swinesherd appearing to be the largest at 251 acres in 1851 and 277 acres in 1871. Nunnery and Newtown Farm were both of a similar size at 175 acres and 180 acres. These three farms would have been run on a similar basis, whereas Hornhill Farm was the smallest. At only 11 acres Hornhill was more of a smallholding. It was rented mainly by families who already had businesses (John Tustin ran a haulier company and in 1911 Jesse Turner, a butcher and farmer was living there.) The land would have been used to raise some livestock to supplement income and provide food and produce for the family. At times the farm was rented by other farmers such as The Watson brothers of Swinesherd, and then incorporated into the larger farms. At these times the house was probably rented out separately.

The three big farms seemed to focus on cattle but were still mixed use. A clue as to the variety of produce produced by the farms is provided by old OS maps. The Ordinance Survey Map from 1890 clearly shows two large orchards adjacent to Newtown Grange, another large

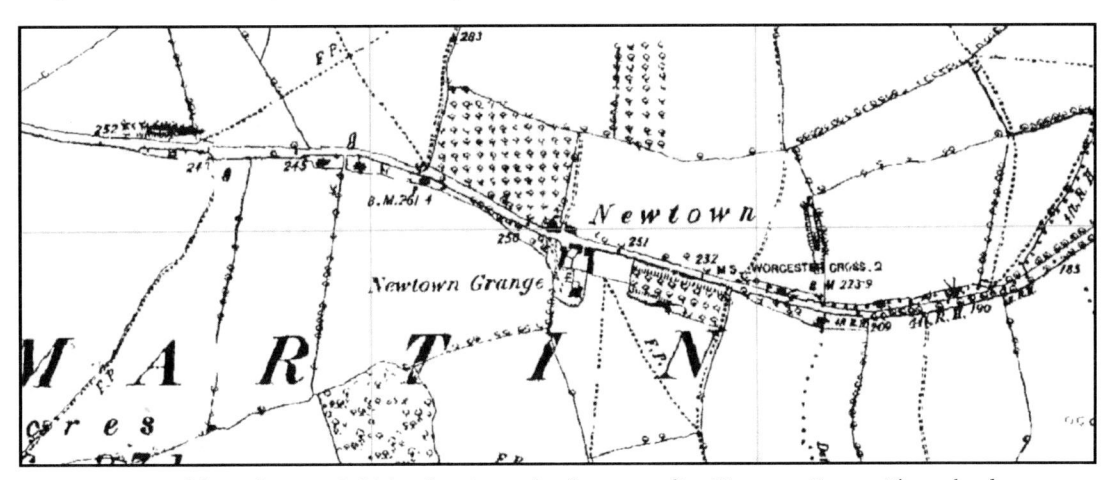

Fig. 53: Detail from the 1890 O.S Map showing orchards surrounding Newtown Grange. The orchard trees are marked in straight rows.

orchard adjacent to Swinesherd Mill and a smaller orchard next to Nunnery Farm. We also know Hornhill Farm had a small garden orchard, as this still remains to this day in Hornhill Meadows on the eastern side of Worcester Woods Country Park and is currently undergoing restoration. Other crops were also grown with various mentions of swede theft from Nunnery Farm, and of game poaching and fruit scrumping from all of the farms often appearing in the reports of petty sessions in the local newspapers. (The Petty Sessions was where court cases that dealt with small crimes like poaching, and acts of theft were tried. These were published in the newspaper regularly and give an interesting snapshot of life as it was then!).

Although all three of the large farms had prize winning cattle, there were also pigs kept (a large swine fever outbreak occurred at Nunnery Farm in 1902) and domestic fowl. Horses were also a vital part of farming and would have been stabled on the farms, and looked after by the 'horseman', who was often classed as the most senior of the farm servants. Horsemanship was a serious business and if horses went lame then the farmers couldn't work. Several cases of horse mistreatment were raised by the farmers and appeared in the Petty Sessions with people being fined as a result. A blacksmith provided a vital service to farmers, as horses needed regular shoeing etc. A blacksmith existed until at least the 1950s on Spetchley Road near Spetchley Gardens. A photo of it can be seen here.

Photo © JB Buckle

Fig. 54: Blacksmith on Spetchley Road in 1961[91].

Horse power started to lessen as steam power became part of the farming revolution. The Watson Brothers at Swinesherd were particular champions of steam with their steam powered cornmill and John Green of Newtown Grange clubbed together with the Watsons and another farmer to set up the 'Newtown Steam Ploughing Company' and buy a steam plough.

Horses continued to be used in farming until after WWII when they were phased out in favour of motor vehicles. The advent of the motor vehicle caused its own problems. Faster vehicles sometimes didn't mix well with farmers driving livestock up public roads. An article in 1910[69] tells of a car running into three of George Pitcher's cattle, which were being herded down the road at the time. The car injured one cow so badly it had to be put down. The other two cattle survived with less severe injuries. The driver refused to give his name and address but was eventually tracked down and fined £5. In 1915 another mishap occurred. George Pitcher was out walking his two fox hound puppies when one was run over by a man called Frederick Frank Kendle from Pershore Garage, who was said to be driving at the rate of 40 miles an hour. The defendant ended up being fined two guineas[70].

By the end of the 19th century things were rapidly starting to change in this part of Worcester. The area, known at the time by the ward name St Martins, was starting to feel the expansion of the railways. When the railways first came to Worcester, it would have been a positive thing for the farmers, who were suddenly able to ship produce far and wide by train to new markets, with little worry of the produce perishing before being sold. The railways expanded, and by the late 1890s early 1900s more cottages were being built in the area, mostly housing railway workers and their families. The value of land started to climb as the city of Worcester expanded. Initially this area was rural. An outlier to the city consisting of a cluster of small hamlets, that lined the main roads heading into Worcester. As the railways grew and the city expanded the farmers started selling off bits of land. Newtown and Nunnery Farms sold off fields which later formed part of the isolation hospital (now Worcestershire Royal Hospital). By the early 1900s the farms were starting to shrink and eventually development proved to be the death knell for the three bigger farms.

Staff and families.

The large farms employed men and boys to work the land, directed by the farmers, whilst the farmers' wives would have taken charge of the domestic duties and employed female servants to assist with running the households. The farmers' families were important and they worked together, often involving several generations, to manage the farms. The farms were headed by the men but the women played a very important but often overlooked role. I use the word 'overlooked' as when doing research into these subjects it is often very hard to find out information about the female members of the farming households. There are small mentions of Charlotte Alice Smith of Newtown Grange giving apples to the poorhouse at Christmas and also cooking for and entering the village show. The life of a farmer's wife was seldom easy unless you were a gentlemen farmer's wife. It is unlikely that our farms were big enough or lucrative enough to employ gentlemen farmers (Gentlemen farmer refers to a breed of farmer who just oversaw the farm without actually getting their hands dirty or doing any physical work). They became a phenomenon during the boom period from the mid-1800s until the farming crash of the mid

1870s, and often became the subject of satire in society at the time. Farmers would have been out every day overseeing their men and working alongside them. Their wives would have been at the farm cooking, making butter, washing and supervising their families, which were often large, and also overseeing livestock. Quite often the farm workers lived on the farms they worked on and the farmers' wives would have been cooking food for them, which the family and workers would have eaten together in the farmhouse kitchen, often sitting together, in front of the range. Some farm workers lived in the farm outbuildings. Others had cottages provided as part of their jobs. This meant that when farm labourers moved job or lost a job, they had to move house and they and their families could become homeless.

An advert in the Worcestershire Chronicle in 1872[71] states *'Wanted a good farm labourer. One who can build and thatch ricks. Must have a good character. A good cottage and garden with liberal wages.'* The labourer was wanted for Nunnery Farm.

Another advert in the Worcestershire Chronicle in 1878[72] asks for *'A good farm labourer who understands barking and working up coppice wood.'* The advert was for Nunnery Farm. Again a cottage and garden were offered as part of the job. This shows that the farm labourers on Nunnery Farm were also working on harvesting the produce from Nunnery Wood (barking was the removal of bark in the tanning process and coppicing is the cutting of trees for rods and poles).

As well as running the households, the farmers' wives were expected to produce many children who would also work on the farms. George Pitcher's (1870–1941) wife, Sarah, had at least nine children. The farms were always left to the eldest son who normally carried their father's name, hence the many generations of George Pitcher, and Edwin and John Watsons!

Crime

Crime was common but most of it was of a petty nature. Several articles appear in the Worcester County Petty Sessions about people stealing swedes from Nunnery Farm. An incident in 1885[73] had three children, aged ten, nine and eight, caught stealing 14lb of swedes. The parents of the children ended up being cautioned and had to pay a fine. Another incident in 1902 had a warrant issued for a boy who had been caught stealing pears from an orchard belonging to Mr Herbert Somer (John Herbert) of Newtown Grange[74]. He was caught and fined 5 shillings. Orchard theft was common. In 1896 three men were caught stealing pears from an orchard belonging to George Pitcher of Nunnery Farm[75].

Stealing game was also very common. In 1875 several men were caught trespassing on land belonging to Edwin Watson of Swinesherd for the purpose of poaching game[76]. The gamekeeper recognised one man who was given a six week prison sentence. Another incident happened in

1875. Two men were caught in a field full of George Pitcher's swedes using dogs to steal game. One man ended up with a fine whilst the other man managed to get discharged[77].

These types of crime were common. People were poor and the reason for theft was often to feed hungry families, or to sell the produce to make a small amount of money.

It was quite common for children to be brought before the courts for petty theft of game and crops. The children were seldom sent to prison, normally being fined. But if the fines weren't paid then a stint of hard labour in prison often ensued and as the children were from very poor families (hence why they were often caught stealing food) they sometimes ended up in jail for short periods.

Farm workers, especially gamekeepers would have patrolled at night to keep an eye out for poachers and thieves and this would have been a never ending task.

Even the farmers themselves weren't above breaking the law. George Pitcher was fined £80 in 1902 for failing to report an outbreak of swine fever that left 129 pigs dead[45].

In 1927 John Somer was fined £1 for selling coloured milk[78]. This was done to make it appear a lot richer than it actually was. John Somer denied all the claims and stated the milk was an odd colour due to the cows recently having calves.

Rural crime is still a problem, even today, but it gives us a valuable record of what was happening on these farms in the past.

Industrial Accidents

Farming was a very dangerous occupation and industrial accidents were common. Many people who worked on farms were injured and sometimes killed in the days before workplace safety legislation. John Watson was run over with his own cart at Swinesherd in 1840 breaking his leg in two places[60]. Horse and Cart accidents were often mentioned, with one of George Pitcher's waggoners Hugh Stanley, being run over by his own cart whilst trying to calm his horse, again causing a broken leg and other injuries[79]. Occasionally the accidents were a lot more serious. In 1857 William Hunt, who was driving a waggon for George Pitcher, ran over and killed a five year old boy on London Road[80]. Another incident in 1914 had John Soloman Tustin, son of John Tustin who farmed at Hornhill and then Ronkswood Farm, thrown from his horse and killed when he fell under a traction engine[81]. If you weren't killed outright, it must be remembered that medicine was nowhere near as advanced as it is now. A broken leg often meant that the leg was set crookedly, resulting in a lifelong limp, and, also, most people did not get sick pay! Accidents could often lead to dismissal from a job and loss of the housing that went with the job, so an accident could be a disaster for families if the main breadwinner was put out of action.

Other types of accident which were common on farms were farm fires. Farms consisted of many wooden, often poorly constructed buildings. When you add in large ricks of hay and straw and lots of farm workers who smoked then disaster often struck.

In 1864 the Birmingham Post reported a large fire at Nunnery Farm[82]. It was stated that *'George Pitcher, supervising the erection of a rick of barley one evening, a barn adjacent was found on fire. Fire engines were sent but a recent drought had dried out adjacent ponds so there was no water.'*

The fire had serious consequences with the flames destroying a barley rick, two straw ricks, a barn, a shed and a number of agricultural implements. The house was lucky to survive and the news article stated that *'the heat had cracked the glass and windows in the main dwelling house and at one time the house was in great peril.'* The fire was said to have been started by some men smoking pipes in the barn.

Another fire affected the Watson Brothers of Swinesherd in 1900. As previously mentioned the fire occurred at Aston Hall in White Ladies Aston where the Watson brothers were doing some work at the time[67]. The Norwich Union fire brigade turned out with a steamer and *'upon arrival found the buildings constructed of brick, timber and thatch consisting of a barn, cattle sheds and three cottages, burnt to the ground. The cottagers saved most of their effects but a threshing machine and straw trusser belonging to Messrs Watson Bros of Swinesherd were destroyed and also two waggons, the produce of about 35 acres of oats and a quantity of straw.'* The fire was a result of arson with the culprit being apprehended the next morning.

Insurance was available and the article mentions that the tenant at Aston Hall farm was insured, but only the wealthier farmers could afford it. As farming equipment and even erection of buildings was down to the tenants, they often lost a lot in farm fires.

George Pitcher (1871-1940) who farmed Nunnery Farm, is probably the best example we have of one of 'our' farmers whose life was irrevocably changed by an industrial accident when he lost his right hand in a swede cutting machine in 1901[43]. Like all of our farmers who survived industrial accidents he continued farming despite his disability. Farming is still ranked to this day as the most dangerous occupation, but in the Victorian and Edwardian eras it was far more deadly and industrial accidents were a common part of farming life.

Modern Day

After several years of planning, Christchurch College finally leased Nunnery Wood to Hereford and Worcestershire County Council on the 26th Oct 1979[3]. This was parcelled together with Perry Wood and the big field adjacent to the current Countryside Centre and together they formed the beginnings of Worcester Woods Country Park.

In its initial stages the formation of the Country Park came with challenges. A paragraph in the 1986 Management Plan[93] for the Country Park sheds light on some of the issues faced and how these issues were ingrained in history.

'It is worth drawing out some of the points made in the study to show that many of the issues facing the area today, have a long antecedence. The problem of illegal woodcutting for instance was so acute in the 17th Century that Christchurch College, then as now owners of Nunnery Wood had to resort to Court action and injunction to prevent further deterioration.'

The management plan also stated; *'in 1847 it is recorded with respect to Nunnery that owing to the nearness of the wood to the town there (were) many depredations committed on it, so that it is necessary to keep a man to look after the wood.'*

Illegal wood cutting was a problem in the early 1980s in Nunnery Woods. I interviewed an ex-Nunnery High School Teacher who mentioned the problem during the Worcester Woods Oral History Recording Project. The teacher, Karen Humphries, had worked at the school since the late 1970s and she regularly worked with pupils doing extra-curricular work in Nunnery Wood in the early 1980s. She said that the rangers came up with an innovative solution to the wood theft problem. They needed a lot of invasive sycamore removed from the south-west corner of the wood, so it was agreed that if the students only removed the marked trees they could keep the firewood! Karen stated that the policy seemed to be a success and resulted in a lot less theft of firewood from Nunnery Wood. According to the 1986 Management Plan[93] a Manpower Services Commission Team was brought in in 1981 to undertake restoration of Nunnery Wood. The wood was thought to have been neglected since the 1930s with the exception of the clear felling in 1946. Coppicing of hazel was resumed in 1981. This is a form of removing hazel understory (shrub sized trees). It then regrows to form straight rods and poles which are used to make woven hurdles and fences. Coppicing is done on a rotation to produce a crop and is traditionally how woodlands have been managed for thousands of years. The coppicing is now undertaken on a more formal basis with two areas cut every winter on a six year rotation. Coppicing is very beneficial to wildlife in woodlands giving a more mixed habitat which flora and fauna thrive in.

In 1985 Hereford and Worcestershire County Council formally declared Worcester Woods a Country Park.

Two years later the Countryside Centre was completed and opened in the summer of 1987. A Property Services Departmental report[92] from Worcestershire County Council in 1987 stated *'The most important and exciting event of the year was the official opening of the Countryside Centre on the 17th July 1987 by Sir Derek Barter, chairman of the Countryside Commission and Miss Audrey Lees on behalf of the chairman of the Nature Conservancy Council.'*

For the opening ceremony five Local Nature Reserves were designated which included Nunnery Wood, Queenswood, Broadmoor Common, Perry Wood and Hartlebury Common. A Ranger post was also added at Worcester Woods Country Park.

Seeing the wood through the trees

Exhibitions which show that there is a great deal more to woodlands than just trees will be staged at Worcestershire's first custom-built countryside centre.

Opened earlier this month the centre is the most ambitious project of its kind undertaken by Hereford-Worcester County Council and provides a valuable link between those who manage the county's country parks and the community.

Built at a cost of £140,000, £70,000 of which came from the Countryside Commission, the bungalow style centre stands on the edge of Worcester Woods Country Park, close to the County Council HQ at Nunnery Wood.

Its object is to encourage greater use and understanding of the countryside and already a year-round programme of seasonal displays has been planned.

"The main aim of the centre is to interpret not only Worcester Woods Country Park, but the countryside as a whole so that people can enjoy it to the full," said Senior Ranger John Williams, who is in charge of the operation.

"We want to educate people but we want them to see how much more there is to woodlands than just the trees.

"We shall have a series of exhibitions highlighting various aspects of the countryside but we also plan to have a permanent display showing the way in which we manage the woodlands and explaining why we do certain things."

An information desk manned by volunteers will provide a back-up for the exhibitions and visitors will be able to buy books on natural history and collect literature on other aspects of the countryside. They will also receive information on other country parks and picnic sites in the county.

Designed by Worcester architects Martin and Nicolette Baines, the centre offers plenty of scope for exhibitions and for the sale of souvenirs offered by country-related organisations and the work of local craftsmen.

An important feature of the building is a 40-seater lecture theatre, complete with projection equipment. Fully equipped, it has been planned to meet the needs of any local group or organisation arranging a film show, talk or minor exhibition.

Free to organisations the theatre will also be made available for a fee to commercial enterprises.

A snack bar will be opened shortly and future plans include a picnic area and children's playground.

"We want people to make sure of the centre and to realise that it is here for the benefit of the community," Mr Williams added.

"There is a fairly large area at the back and we hope to use this to stage displays of country crafts such as horse-shoeing, wattle making and all activities related to woodlands."

It is due to be formally opened on July 17 by Countryside Commission chairman Sir Derek Barber and the chairman of the Nature Conservancy Council Mr William Wilkinson.

ANN WATKIN

● Assistant Countryside Officer Robert Wilkins (centre), with Bret Westwood (exhibition consultant) and Pam Stubbs (interpretation officer) showing some of the exhibits on display in the new Worcester Countryside Centre

Fig. 55: Article in the Berrows Worcester Journal about the opening of the Countryside Centre in 1987[95].

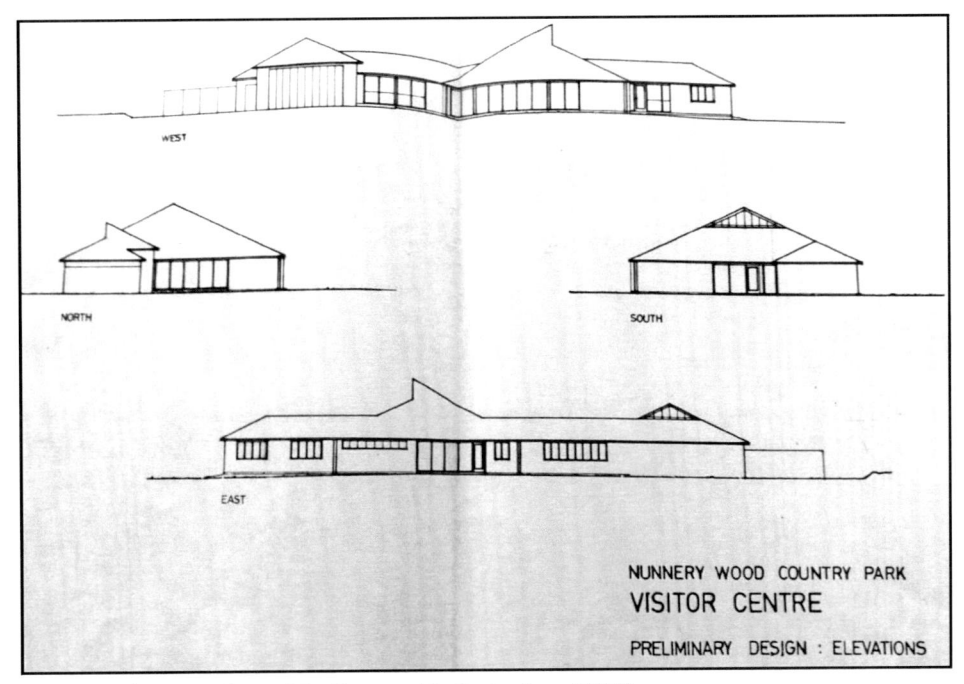

Fig. 56: Preliminary plans of the Countryside Centre from 1986[92].

Fig. 57: An event outside the new Countryside Centre (no date). Credit Countryside Service, Worcestershire County Council.

At the time Perry Wood was still included in the Country Park although it has always been separated by a housing estate. In 1987 both woods were declared Local Nature Reserves (LNR's) giving them conservation and planning protection. It was envisaged that Warndon Wood and Tolladine Wood would also be added to the Country Park[3], and green links would spread out from the central site linking the four woods together, hence the name Worcester Woods Country Park. Unfortunately this plan never came into fruition and in 2004 Perry Wood went back to being managed separately by Worcester City Council whilst Nunnery Wood remained the sole wood in Worcester Woods Country Park, which to this day is still managed by Worcestershire County Council.

In 1990 Worcester Woods Country Park gained more land in the form of Hornhill Meadows. The meadows, previously part of Hornhill Farm were purchased from a Mr Tupper on the 20th

May 1990[3]. The field to the far east of the meadows, formerly part of Swinesherd Farm was also purchased on the 5th April 1990. Some land was also added to the south of Hornhill meadows at roughly the same time. This particular field, also previously part of Swinesherd Farm was surfaced with several small hills and slopes and was designed as a mountain bike area. This idea never took hold and today it has fruit trees planted on its lower slopes and is grazed by cattle as meadow land.

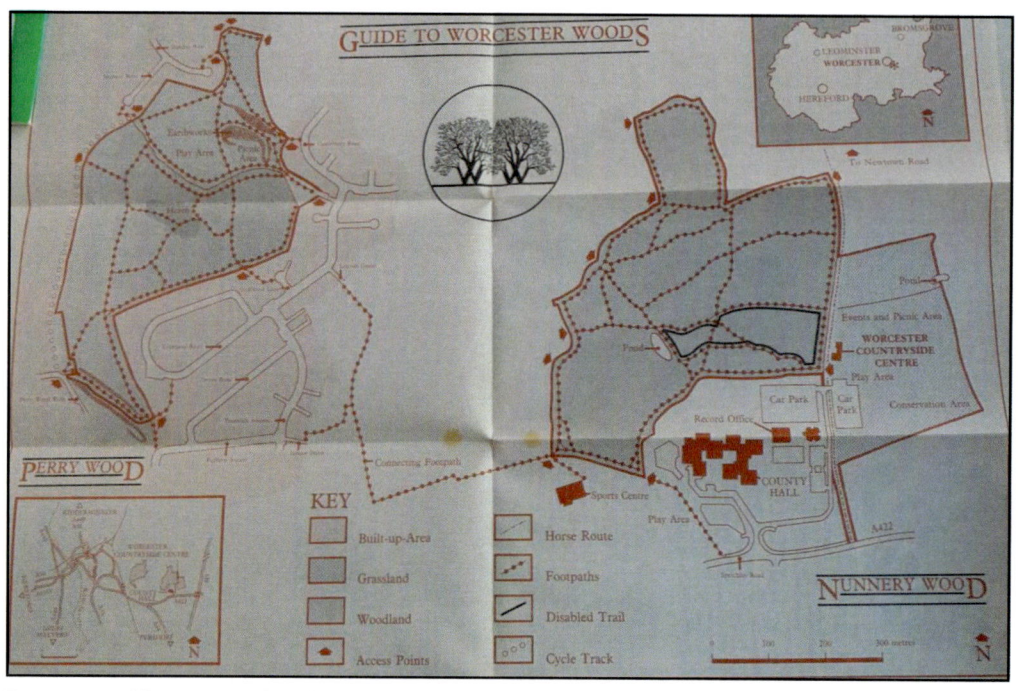

Fig. 58: An old country park leaflet dated from the 1990s showing Perry Wood along with Nunnery Wood forming part of Worcester Woods Country Park.

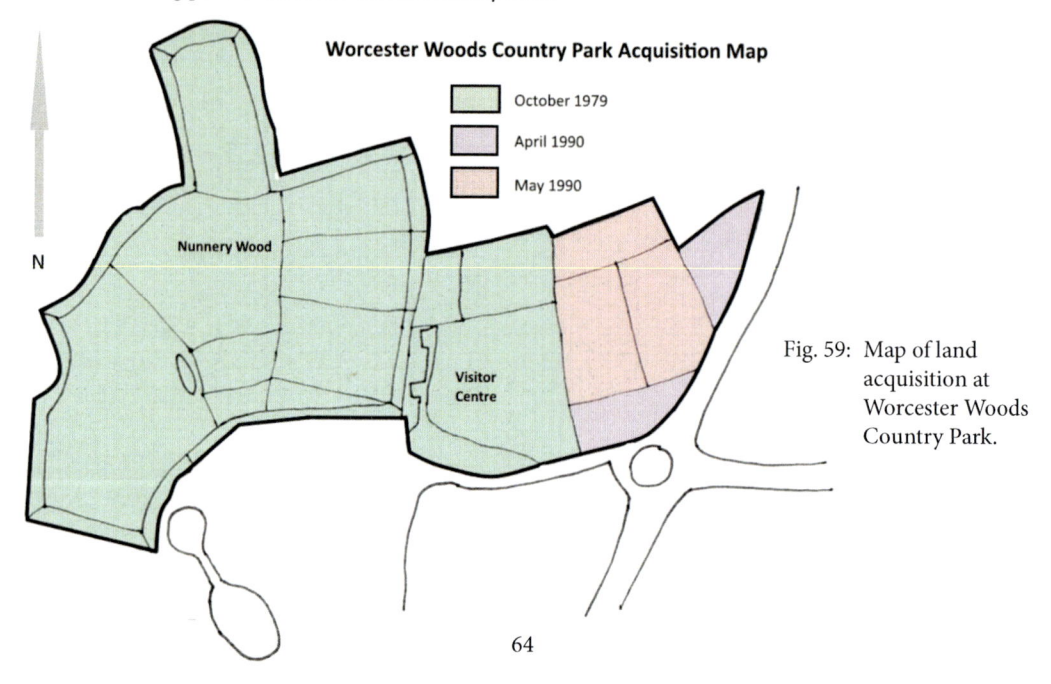

Fig. 59: Map of land acquisition at Worcester Woods Country Park.

Hornhill Meadows received its Local Nature Reserve designation in 1994 and has since been managed as meadow land to encourage the rare wildflowers. Cattle grazing was reintroduced in 2003 to help manage the meadow and benefit the wildflowers. Cattle still graze these fields today.

The car park was expanded in the early 1990s with land across Wildwood Drive being used as a coach park and overflow car park. At the time Worcester Woods Country Park was hosting a hugely popular car boot sale and according to visitor statistics in the 1993 management plan[96] 316,000 people participated in the event between June 1989 and October 1990 making up 75% of all visits to the park!

The car boot sale remained in place until 2004 when its impact on the park necessitated moving it to a more appropriate location. The land on the other side of Wildwood Drive, which was used as an overflow car park and coach bay, was then given to the St Richards Hospice charity and is now the location of the current hospice building.

Since then, further building works have occurred around the park with it being developed on all sides. Worcester Woods Country Park now remains as a green oasis on the edge of Worcester City and will remain with its rich history for future generations to enjoy.

Fig. 60: Inside the Countryside Centre. No date given but likely to be 1980s or 1990s. Credit Countryside Service.

Fig. 61: Another view inside The Countryside Centre of the birdwatching station. No date given. Credit Countryside Service. Worcestershire County Council.

Fig. 62: The Countryside Centre. Likely taken in late 1990s. Credit Countryside Service. Worcestershire County Council.

Fig. 63: Entrance to Nunnery Wood. Likely taken late 1990s. Credit Countryside Service. Worcestershire County Council.

References

1. Wardle T, Historic Worcestershire Streets (2014)
2. Hopper B, Farms of Eastern Worcester (2012)
3. Worcester Woods Management Plan (1993) Planning Division, Hereford and Worcester County Council.
4. The Victoria History of the Counties of England, Worcestershire, (reprinted 1971 based on 1913 edition) University of London Institute of Historical Research.
5. Survey at Worcester Woods Country Park, Worcester. A Mindykowski, J Bretherton. (2004) Historic Environment and Archaeology Service.
6. Worcestershire Archives 1814 plan Nunnery Wood BA9642/13.
7. Worcestershire Archives 1790 Map Land belonging to Mr Russell BA 1638/27
8. Worcestershire Archives 1824 Road Map around Nunnery Wood BA 438/22
9. Worcestershire Archives 1838/9 Map Swinesherd Farm BA 4383
10. Worcestershire Archives Newtown Grange 1867 auction notice and map BA4627
11. Worcestershire Archives Nunnery Farm 1836 poster of sale, BA 3762/8 vol iii pp74.
12. Worcestershire Archives Lord and Parker Collection BA 1638
13. Worcestershire Archives leaflets and arm bands relating to Worcester Woods Country Park BA 12649/1
14. Worcestershire Archives Plans of The Countryside Centre 1986 BA 10125/4
15. Worcestershire Archives Particulars and Conditions of Sale (field belonging to George Pitcher) 1918 BA 9360/CAB/23/142.
16. Worcestershire Archives Minutes of General Purposes Committee 1937-1948 minutes BA 11241 box 5.
17. Worcestershire Archives 1938 Map Nunnery Farm and Sale transfer of Nunnery Farm documents BA 9360/CAB 23/58 Part A.
18. Worcester Journal 20th April 1826. Sale of Hornhill Farm.
19. UK City and County Directories, Worcester 1855.
20. Worcestershire Chronicle 1857, 20th May. Hornhill Farm for sale.
21. 1879 Littlebury's Directory and Gazetteer of Worcester and District, Ballentyne, Hanson and Co.
22. Worcestershire Chronicle 16th Aug 1884 Hornhill Farm Sold.
23. 1885 in the Worcester Journal Dec 12th. Hornhill House.
24. Worcestershire Chronicle 20th Aug 1892. Hornhill House Auction Report.
25. Worcester Journal Nov 4th 1813, Reward for stolen cow.
26. Worcester Journal 12th August 1813, Nunnery Farm Auction.
27. Worcester Journal 19th May 1814, Auction of part of Nunnery Farm.
28. Hereford Journal 22nd Aug 1821. Nunnery Farm for Sale.
29. Worcester Journal 22nd April 1824. Nunnery Farm for Sale.
30. Worcester Journal 5th Aug 1824. Nunnery Crops Sale.
31. Worcester Journal in 1826 23rd Nov. Death of W A Oliver.

32 Worcester Journal 5th March 1829. Pig theft from Nunnery Farm.
33 Worcester Journal 15th Nov 1832. Sale of the effects of Mrs Oliver of Nunnery Farm.
34 Worcester Journal December 27th 1884. In Memoriam, Rev William Parker.
35 Ancestry.co.uk Parker Family Tree.
36 Personal notes on the Parker Family provided by Robin Whittaker, ex County Archivist for Worcestershire.
37 Worcester Journal May 27th, 1882, Death of Mr John Parker.
38 Worcestershire Chronicle 3rd May 1890. Death of Mr Francis Parker.
39 Worcestershire Chronicle 12th April 1848. Stealing of Mr Pitchers Sheep.
40 Ancestry.co.uk. Pitcher Family Tree.
41 The Tewkesbury Register and Agricultural Gazette. 27th Jan 1940. Death of George Pitcher.
42 Worcester Journal. 24th Feb 1894. Death of W G Y Pitcher.
43 Worcestershire Chronicle, 23rd March 1901. Accident at Nunnery Farm.
44 Worcestershire Chronicle 30th March 1901. Pershore Parish Council Results.
45 Granthan Journal 8th November 1902. Swinefever Outbreak at Nunnery Farm.
46 Birmingham Daily Post 21st Feb 1922 George Pitcher Waggon Accident.
47 Tewkesbury Register and Agricultural Gazette 16th Feb 1935 Sale of Fowl.
48 Tewksbury Register and Agricultural Gazette, 9th Oct 1948
49 Worcester Journal 19th May 1814 Auction of lots, Nunnery Wood.
50 Worcestershire Chronicle 14th Feb 1880. Damaging underwood in Nunnery Wood.
51 Worcester Journal 13th Jan 1883. Setting snares in Nunnery Wood.
52 Bells Weekly Messenger 25th July 1864 John Green exhibits at the Royal Show.
53 Birmingham Journal 18th July 1863. John Green Exhibits.
54 Worcestershire Chronicle 28th April 1852. Death of Jane Green.
55 Worcestershire Chronicle 16th Nov 1878. Marriage of Thomas Smith to Charlotte Alice Holland.
56 Worcestershire Chronicle 4th Aug 1888. Death of Walter Holland.
57 Worcester Journal 17th Feb 1900. Cattle invading orchard belonging to George Hayes.
58 Ancestry.co.uk Watson Family Tree.
59 Worcester Journal 29th Jan 1846. Sale of the late Mr Watsons effects from Spetchley Farm.
60 Worcester Journal 16th July 1840. John Watson gets injured.
61 Worcester Journal 21st July 1842. Mr Watson donated towards the rebuilding of Whittington Church.
62 Worcestershire Chronicle. 2nd Oct 1861. The steam plough.
63 Bell's Weekly Messenger 14th Nov 1868. Advert for farm bailiff.
64 Worcester Journal 25th Sept 1880. Auction of goods at Swinesherd Farm.
65 Spetchley House, notes from the archivist 2018.
66 Worcestershire Chronicle 11th March 1899. Elections to Whittington Parish Council.
67 Worcestershire Chronicle 17th Nov 1900. Farm fire Aston Hall.
68 Tewkesbury Register and Agricultural Gazette 14th Nov 2018. Sale of mill tools from Swinesherd.
69 Birmingham Daily Gazette 8th Sept 1910 Car runs into George Pitchers cattle.
70 Gloucester Echo 15th Dec 1915. Car runs into George Pitchers dogs.
71 Worcestershire Chronicle   13th March 1872. Advert for farm labourer.
72 Worcestershire Chronicle in 2nd March 1878. Advert for farm labourer.
73 Worcestershire Chronicle 28th March 1885. Swede stealing at Nunnery Farm.

74	Worcestershire Chronicle 22nd Nov 1902. Pear stealing from Newtown.
75	Worcestershire Chronicle 5th sept 1896. Stealing fruit from Nunnery Farm.
76	Worcester Journal 13th Nov 1875. Poaching from Swinesherd Farm.
77	Worcester Journal 18th Sept 1875. Stealing game from George Pitcher's field.
78	Gloucester Citizen 27th Aug 1927. John Somer fined for selling adulterated milk.
79	Worcestershire Chronicle 12 April 1884. Waggon accident.
80	Worcester Herald 19th Sept 1857. George Pitcher's waggoner kills boy.
81	Birmingham Mail Sat 11th July 1914. John Tustin jnr killed falling off his horse.
82	The Birmingham Post 8th August 1864. Fire at Nunnery Farm.
83	Berrows Worcester Journal. 4th Dec 1794. Death of Dorothy Best. Quoted in the Berrows Worcester Journal Dec 1894 in an article called 'Memories from 100 years ago'.
84	Berrows Worcester Journal Feb 26th 1795. Death of Francis Best. Quoted in Berrows Worcester Journal 9th Feb 1895 article called 'Memories from 100 years ago.'
85	Worcestershire Archives. BA1638/63 A map of land adjoining Perry Wood dated 1819 with a watercolour view from Perry Wood towards Worcester.
86	Worcestershire Archives BA 1638 Box 72. Marriage agreement between William Parker and Jane Paget.
87	A History of Worcestershire Agriculture and Rural Revolution, R C Gawt (1939) Littlebury and co lmt.
88	Gloucestershire Archives D2025/box 41/bundle 11. Particulars of sale, The Nunnery, St Martins. 31st May 1834.
89	Berrows Worcester Journal Aug 23rd 1862. Toll court case.
90	Worcestershire Archives. Photo of the M5 bridge being built over Spetchley Road. 1960. BA 743.038. B Buckle.
91	Worcestershire Archives. Old photo of the blacksmiths on Spetchley Road. BA 743:072. 1961. B Buckle.
92	Worcestershire County Council. Property Departmental Report 1987-1988.
93	Worcestershire County Council. Management Plan Worcester Woods Country Park July 1986. (Worcestershire Archives BA 474:03).
94	Worcestershire Archives. 1751 Plan of St Martin. R705:27.
95	Berrows Worcester Journal July 3rd 1987. Seeing the Wood Through the Trees. Countryside Centre Opening Article.
96	Worcestershire County Council 1993 Management Plan for Worcester Woods Country Park. Countryside Service.
97	Greens History of Worcester vol 2. (1796) Valentine Green.
98	Worcesterobserver.co.uk 6th October 2015 'Publicans will is two centuries old' Newspaper online article quoting Bob Blandford.
99	Worcestershire Chronicle 8th Nov 1838. Obituaries.
100	Berrows Worcester Journal. 10th October 1844. 'Sale of Farming Stock.'
101	Kingsbury J G.(1984) Nunnery and Perry Woods, Worcester: Historical Ecology and Land Use Changes. Countryside Service. Hereford and Worcester County Council.
102	Worcestershire Archives. 705:192. Last Will and Testament of George Pitcher. 1940.
103	Berrows Worcester Journal. 24th Feb 1894. William Godwin Yeend Pitcher Obituary.
104	Worcestershire Archives. BA438/22 Tithe Map 1839. St Martins.

Illustrations

Fig. 1: Archaeology map detail. 2004. Reproduced with kind permission from Worcestershire Archive and Archaeology Service. Worcestershire County Council.

Fig. 2: Ridge and furrow illustration.

Fig. 3: Ridge and furrow photo. Jane Pond 2018.

Fig. 4: Ditch and pond photo. 2018. Author's own.

Fig. 5: Ditch and bank boundary. 2018. Author's own.

Fig. 6: Old oak tree. 2019. Author's own.

Fig. 7: Pollarding illustration. Author's own.

Fig. 8: Overview map. The four farms and Worcester Woods Country Park. Author's own.

Fig. 9: Overview map. The four farms; general. Author's own.

Fig. 10: Worcester Woods Country Park location. 1890 O.S map reproduced courtesy of The Ordnance Survey.

Fig. 11: Hornhill Farm location detail. 1890 O.S map. Reproduced courtesy of The Ordnance Survey.

Fig. 12: Photo of wall and ditch by the Hornhill House remains. 2018. Author's own.

Fig. 13: Photo of the rubble remains of Hornhill House. 2018. Jane Pond.

Fig. 14: Photo of a chain harrow found at Hornhill. 2005. Credit Jane Pond.

Fig. 15: Picture of Nunnery Farmhouse. Copyright Marion Feasey.

Fig. 16: Detail Nunnery Farm Map.

Fig. 17: Detail from 1751 map. Reproduced with kind permission from the Worcestershire Archives.

Fig. 18: Detail from 1790 map. Hill family. Reproduced with kind permission from the Worcestershire Archives.

Fig. 19: Detail from 1824 map showing Nunnery Farm. Reproduced with kind permission from the Worcestershire Archives.

Fig. 20: Copy of 1824 map. Nunnery Farm and the Ronkswood Estate. Reproduced with kind permission from the Worcestershire Archives.

Fig. 21: Nunnery Farm Estate notice of sale 1836. Reproduced with kind permission from the Worcestershire Archives.

Fig. 22: Nunnery Farm map. 1850s with field names.

Fig. 23: Photo of Little Comberton Church. 2018. Courtesy of Jane Pond.

Fig. 24: Photo of the winding mechanism of the Little Comberton Church clock. 2018. Author's own.

Fig. 25: Photo of the bells at Little Comberton Church. 2018. Author's own.

Fig. 26: picture of the view towards Worcester from Redhill. Reproduced with kind permission from the Worcestershire Archives.

Fig. 27: Photo of Woodside House. 2019. Author's own.

Fig. 28: Photo of the Pitcher Family. 1892. Reproduced courtesy of Robert and Beth Low.

Fig. 29: Detail of Nunnery Farm map. Piece above the wood.

Fig. 30: Example of George Pitcher's handwriting. Reproduced with kind permission from the Worcestershire Archives.

Fig. 31: Old photo of Jane Rushton. No date. Reproduced with kind permission fromTessa Kay.

Fig. 32: Detail of George Pitcher. 1892. Reproduced with king permission from Robert and Beth Low.

Fig. 33: Photo of Nunnery Cottage. 2019. Author's own.

Fig. 34: Old photo of Nunnery Cottage. No date. Reproduced with kind permission from Tessa Kay.

Fig. 35: Photo of Nunnery Farmhouse. Dated 1951. Reproduced courtesy of Jim Bishop.

Fig. 36: Photo of tractor at Nunnery Farm dated 1951. Reproduced courtesy of Jim Bishop.

Fig. 37. Photo of barn at Nunnery Farm. Dated 1951. Reproduced courtesy of Jim Bishop.

Fig. 38: Photo of fire engine at Nunnery Farm. 1951. Reproduced courtesy of Jim Bishop.

Fig. 39: Illustration of the changing shape of Nunnery Wood.

Fig. 40: Photo of location for Newtown Grange on Newtown Road. 2019. Author's own.

Fig. 41: Newtown Grange layout map with field names.

Fig. 42: Photo of plaque at St Martins Church in remembrance of John Green and his wives. 2018. Jane Pond.

Fig. 43: Auction notice Newtown Grange. Reproduced with kind permission from the Gloucestershire Archives.

Fig. 44: Photo of Walter Holland Portrait. 2019. Author's own.

Fig. 45: Photo of George Hitchins outhouse on Newtown Road. 2019. Author's own.

Fig. 46: Photo of the Cornmill house at Swinesherd.2019. Author's own.

Fig. 47: Swinesherd Farm map with field names.

Fig. 48: Photo of Fowlers steam engine and plough. 2019. Author's own.

Fig. 49: O.S map 1890. Swinesherd Farm and orchard detail. Reproduced courtesy of the Ordnance Survey.

Fig. 50: Photo of John Watson memorial plaque at All Saints Church. 2018. Reproduced courtesy of Jane Pond.

Fig. 51: Photo of gravestone. Marian Watson. 2018. Author's own.

Fig. 52: Photo Motorway bridge construction at Swinesherd. 1960. B Buckle.

Fig. 53: O.S map detail. 1890. Orchards at Newtown Grange. Reproduced courtesy of the Ordnance Survey.

Fig. 54: Photo of a blacksmiths at Spetchley Road. B Buckle.

Fig. 55: Newspaper Article. 'Seeing the Wood Through the Trees' opening of the Countryside Centre. Reproduced with kind permission from Berrows Worcester Journal.

Fig. 56: Preliminary plans of the Countryside Centre 1986. Reproduced Courtesy of Property Services. Worcestershire County Council.

Fig. 57: Photo of the Countryside Centre. No date. Reproduced with kind permission from the Countryside Service. Worcestershire County Council.

Fig. 58: Photo of an old Worcester Woods Country Park leaflet dated 1990s. Author's own.

Fig. 59: Worcester Woods Country Park acquisition map.

Fig. 60: Photo of spider display inside the Countryside Centre. No date. Reproduced courtesy of the Countryside Service. Worcestershire County Council.

Fig. 61: Photo of display inside the Countryside Centre. No date. Reproduced courtesy of the Countryside Service. Worcestershire County Council.

Fig. 62: Photo of the Countryside Centre in the late 1990s. reproduced courtesy of the Countryside Service. Worcestershire County Council.

Fig. 63: Photo of the entrance to Nunnery Wood. Late 1990s. reproduced courtesy of the Countryside Service. Worcestershire County Council.

Fig. 64: Photo of the Worcester Woods Country Park sites team. 2019. Author's own.

The Current Worcester Woods Country Park sites team.
From the left Maurice Jones, Tanya Feasey, Rob Stevenson and John Clarke.

Thank you!

Thank you to everyone who has helped with the production of this book! Special thanks go to Jane Pond for help in the archives and coming on numerous trips around graveyards, churches etc. Thanks to Robin Whittaker who offered lots of valuable advice and pointers and answered all of my questions with great patience. Thanks to Karen Humphries, Maurice Jones, Phil Williams and Jim Bishop for your memories. Thanks to Laura Pitt for lots of help with research, enquiries and listening politely whilst I talked about history a lot! Thanks to David and Marion Feasey for the illustrations and help with proof reading. Thank you to Karen Davidson from the Spetchley Archives. Thanks to Worcestershire County Council's Countryside Service for all the help with documents, maps etc. And a big thank you to Worcestershire Archives who tirelessly answered so many enquiries and helped locate documents etc. And a huge thank you to all the other people who helped send in pictures, gave me advice, support and much more!

Copyright

Every effort has been made to trace copy right owners and gain permission for the pictures within this book. If you think you are the holder of copy right for pictures within this book and haven't been credited then please get in touch with the author who will be happy to rectify the situation.